BECOMES EXPERT IN CYBERSECURITY

KUNAL MAURYA

Contents

I

BEING A HACKER

1.1 Resources

This lesson is about how to learn – a critical skill for a hacker. Hacking, in reality, is a creative process that is based more on lifestyle than lesson. We can't teach you everything that you need to know, but we can help you recognize what you need to learn. This is also true due to the constant advances in the computer sciences. What we teach today may not be relevent tomorrow. It is much better for you to embrace hacker learning habits, which are probably the most vital part of hacking and will separate you from the script kiddie (a person who runs hacking tools without knowing how or why they work). Words and concepts you don't understand in this workbook may require research on the web or in a library. If you don't understand a word or a topic, it is essential you look it up. Ignoring it will only make it difficult for you to understand concepts in other workbooks. The other workbooks may ask you to investigate a topic on the web and then expect you to use the information that you find on the web to complete the exercises in that workbook – but those workbooks won't explain to you how to do this research. This workbook is the only one with a thorough explanation of how to research built into it, so be sure to spend as much time as you need to learn how to research using the various resources available to you. Don't just limit yourself to computers, hacking, and the internet. Great hackers are well arounded and creative. Many of them are painters, writers, and designers. Hacking skills can also be applied to other fields, such as Political Science (see The Prince by Machiavelli for an example). Besides being interested in other fields, you should be interested in how other businesses operate. Reading books on everything from psychology to science fiction will make you a much more versatile and functional hacker. Remember, hacking is about figuring out how things work regardless of how they were designed to work. This is how you expose insecurities, vulnerabilities, and leaks.

1.1.1 Books

Books are a great way to learn the foundation and factual science of all that you are willing to explore. Want to know something about the fundamentals of a science, like the hardware details of your PC? Nothing will help you more than reading a current book on the subject. The main problem with books for computers is that they quickly become old. The secret is to learn to see the fundamental structure underneath the thin skin of details. MS-DOS and Windows are clearly different, but both are based on principles of Boolean logic that have driven computers since Ada, Countess of Lovelace, wrote the first computer programs in the nineteenth century. Security and privacy concerns may have changed in the last 2,500 years, but The Art of War by Sun Tzu covers fundamental principles that still apply today. Even though information found in books may not be as 'up to date' as information that comes from other sources, you will find that the information you find in books is more likely to be factually accurate than that which comes from other sources. A writer spending a year writing a book is more likely to check facts than someone who is updating a blog six times a day. (See Section 1.1.3 Zines and Blogs for more information.) But remember – accurate does not mean unbiased. It's not necessary to start a library of your own, but you may want to write notes in margins or otherwise mark what you read, and this is something you can only do in your own books. Finally, don't look at a book and give up before you even start just because of the size and complexity. Most of these massive tomes that you see sitting around are not read from cover to cover. Think of them as prehistoric web pages. Open one up to random page and begin to read. If you don't understand something, go backward and look for the explanation (or skip forward to something that does make sense). Jump through the book, backwards and forwards, just as you would bounce from link to link in a web page. This type of non-linear reading is often much more interesting and satisfying for hackers, as it's about satisfying curiosity more than it is about "reading".

1.1.2 Magazines and Newspapers

The use of magazines and newspapers is highly encouraged for providing concise, timely information. However, magazines are usually short on details and often focus too much on the zeitgeist of the community. This is something that a hacker needs to know – social engineering and password cracking, in particular, are more effective if you have a solid grounding in pop culture – but you also need to know that 'pop journalism' isn't always 'accurate journalism'. Another issue you should consider is the topic or theme of the magazine. A Linux magazine will attempt to down-play Microsoft Windows, because it is a conflicting theme and that is what their main readers want to read. The best way to combat these two flaws is by being well and widely read. If you read an interesting fact in a magazine, look into it further. Pretend that you believe it, and look for confirmations, then pretend that you don't believe it, and look for rebuttals. Exercises: A. Search the Web for 3 online magazines regarding Security. B. How did you find these magazines? C. Are all three magazines about computer security?

1.1.3 Zines and Blogs

Zines are small, often free magazines that have a very small distribution (less than 10,000 readers) and are often produced by hobbyists and amateur journalists. Zines, like the famous 2600 zine or Phrack Hacking web zine, are written by volunteers and the producers do not edit the content for non-technical errors. This means the language can be harsh for those not anticipating such writing. Zines have a very strong theme and are very opinionated. However, they are more likely to show and argue both sides, as they do not care to nor have to appease advertisers and subscribers. Blogs are a modernization of the zine. Blogs are updated more often and use communities to tie in very strong themes. Like zines, however, anyone may criticize a story and show an opposing opinion. For blogs, it is important to read the commentary just as much as the story.

Exercises:

A. Search the Web for 3 zines regarding computer security.

B. How did you find these zines?

C. Why do you classify these as zines? Remember, just because they market it as a zine or put "zine" in the title does not mean it is one.

D. Search the Web for 3 blogs regarding computer security.

E. What communities are these associated with?

1.1.4 Forums and Mailing

Lists Forums and mailing lists are communally developed media, much like a recording of a series of conversations at a party. The conversations shift focus often, and much of what is said is rumor, and, when the party is over, no one is certain who said what. Forums and mailing lists are similar, because there are many ways for people to contribute inaccurate information – sometimes intentionally – and there are also ways for people to contribute anonymously. And, since topics and themes change quickly, it's important to read the whole thread of comments and not just the first few in order to get the best information.

You can find forums on almost any topic and many online magazines and newspapers offer forums for readers to write opinions regarding published articles. For this case, forums are invaluable for getting more than one opinion on an article, because, no matter how much you liked the article, there is certain to be someone who didn't.

Many mailing lists exist on special topics, but these are hard to find. Often times, you must look for an idea before you find a mailing list community supporting it.

For a hacker, what is most important to know is that many forums and mailing lists are not searchable through major search engines. While you might find a forum or a list through a topic search in a search engine, you may not find information on individual posts. This information is called "the invisible web" as it contains information and data that is invisible to many since a very specific search is needed, often through meta-search engines or only directly on the website of the forum.

Exercises:

A. Find 3 computer security forums.

B. How did you find these forums?

C. Can you determine the whole theme of the website?

D. Do the topics in the forums reflect the theme of the website hosting them?

E. Find 3 computer security mailing lists.

F. Who is the "owner" of these lists?

G. On which list would you expect the information to be more factual and less opinionated and why?

1.1.5 Newsgroups

Newsgroups have been around a long time. There were newsgroups long before the Web existed. Google purchased the entire archive of newsgroups and put them online at http://groups.google.com. You will find posts in there from the early 1990s. This archive is important for finding who is the original owner of an idea or a product. It is also useful for finding obscure information that is perhaps too small a topic for someone to put on a web page. Newsgroups are not used less today than they were years ago, before the web became the mainstream for sharing information. However, they also haven't grown as their popularity is replaced by new web services like blogs and forums.

Exercises:

A. Using Google's groups, find the oldest newsgroup posting you can about security.

B. Find other ways to use newsgroups - are there applications you can use to read newsgroups?

C. How many newsgroups can you find that talk about computer hacking?

1.1.6 Websites

The de facto standard for sharing information is currently through a web browser. While we classify this all as "the web" the real term is "web services," as not everything on the web is a website. If you check e-mail using a web browser, you are using a web service. Often times, web services require privileges. This means you need a login name and password to gain access. Having access and the legal right to access is known as having "privileges". Hacking into a website to allow you to change the page may be having access, but since it is not your legal right to do so, it is not privileged access. We are only concerned with having privileged access, but as your experience grows with using the web, you will find many places give access to privileged areas by accident. As you find this, you should get into the habit of reporting this to the website owner.

Websites are searchable through a large number of search engines. It's even possible to make your own search engine, if you have the time and hard drive space. Often, it's the search engines who get privileged access and pass it on to you. Sometimes it is in the form of cache. A cache is an area of memory on the search engine's server where the search engine stores pages that matched your search criteria. If you click on the link that says cached, instead of the actual link, then you will see a single page that shows what the search engine found during its search. The search engines save this information to prove that the search was valid – if, for instance, a page goes down or is changed between the time that you initiated your search and the time that you try to access the page that was returned – but you can also use the cached pages for other purposes, such as bypassing a slow server. One of the most useful public caches is at http://www.archive.org. Here you will find cached versions of whole websites from over the years.

One final note on websites, do not assume you can trust the content of the websites you visit just because they appear in a search engine. Many hacker attacks and viruses are spread just by visiting a website or downloading programs to run. You can safeguard yourself by not downloading programs from untrusted websites and by making sure the browser you use is up-to-date on security patches.

Exercises:

A. Using a search engine, find sites that may have mistakenly given privileged access to everyone. To do this, we will look for directory listings which are accessible when you don't go directly to the right web page. To do this, we will go to http://www.google.com and enter this into the search box:

allintitle: "index of" .pdf

Click on a link in the results and you should find one that looks like a directory listing.

This type of searching is also known as Google Hacking.

B. Can you find other types of documents in this way using Google? Find 3 more directory listings which contain .xls files and .avi files.

C. There are many search engines out there besides Google. A good researcher knows how to use them all. Some websites specialize in tracking search engines, such as http://www.searchengine.com. However, there are many more and you can generally find them by using search engines. There is even a search engine for "the invisible web". Find 10 search engines which are NOT meta search engines.

D. Search for "security testing and ethical hacking" and list the top 3 answers.

E. Search for the same without the quotes and give the top 3 answers. Are they different?

F. It is very different to search for a topic than it is to search for a word or phrase. In exercise D, you searched for a phrase. Now you will search for an idea. To do this, you need to think about what you want and how you want to find it. For example, you want to find an online resource of magazines for ethical hacking. If you enter online resource of magazines for ethical hacking into a search engine, you will get a number of opinions about the topic. This is helpful but not as helpful as actually getting the resource. Instead, you need to think, "If I was to make such a resource, what information would be in there and what key words could I pick from that information?"

Put the following words and phrases into a search engine and find out which provides the best results for your search:

1. my favorite list of magazines on ethical hacking
2. list of ethical hacking magazines
3. resources for ethical hackers
4. ethical hacking magazine
5. magazines ethical hacking security list resource

G. Find the oldest website from Mozilla in the Internet Archive. To do this you need to search on "www.mozilla.org" at the http://www.archive.org website.

H. Now to put it all together, let's say you want to download version 1 of the Netscape web browser. Using search engines and the Internet Archives, see if you can locate and download version 1 (but don't install it).

1.1.7 Chat

Chats, also known as Internet Relay Chat (IRC), as well as Instant Messaging (IM), are very popular modes of quickly communicating with others. As a research source, chat is extremely inconsistent, because you will be dealing with individuals in real time. Some will be friendly, and some will be rude. Some will be harmless pranksters, but some will be malicious liars. Some will be intelligent and willing to share information, and some will be completely uninformed, but no less willing to share. It can be difficult to know which is which. However, once you get comfortable with certain groups and channels, you may be accepted into the community, and you will be allowed to ask more and more questions, and you will learn who you can trust. Eventually you will be able to learn the very newest security information (also known as zero day, which implies that it was just discovered) and advance your own knowledge.

Exercises:

A. Find 3 chat programs to use for instant messaging. What makes them different? Can they all be used to talk to each other?

B. Find out what IRC is and how you can connect to it. Once you are able to connect, enter the ISECOM chat room as announced on the front page of http://www.isecom.org.

C. How do you know which channels exist to join in IRC? Find 3 computer security channels and 3 hacker channels. Can you enter these channels? Are there people talking or are they "bots"?

1.1.8 P2P

Peer to Peer, also known as P2P, is a network inside the Internet. Instead of many local computers communicating with each other through a centralized, remote computer, the computers in a P2P network communicate directly with each other. Most people associate P2P with the downloading of mp3s and pirated movies, however, many other P2P networks exist – both for the purposes of exchanging a wide variety of information and as a means to conduct research on distributed information sharing. One website dedicated to teaching about this, http://infoanarchy.org, is based on the premise that information should be free. On the Infoanarchy website, you can find a listing of available P2P networks and clients.

The problem with P2P networks is that, while you can find information on just about anything on them, some of that information is on the network illegally. The Hacker Highschool program doesn't condone the use of P2P to illegally download intellectual property, but there is no question that P2P networks can be a vital resource for finding information. Remember: there is nothing illegal about P2P networks – there are a lot of files that are available to be freely distributed under a wide variety of licenses – but there are also a lot of files on these networks that shouldn't be there. Don't be afraid to use P2P networks, but be aware of the dangers.

1.2 Further Lessons

Now you should practice to master the skill of researching. The better you get at it, the more information you can find quickly, and the faster you will learn. To help you become a better researcher for the Hacker Highschool program, here are some additional topics and terms for you to investigate:

Meta Search

II

BASIC COMMANDS IN LINUX AND WINDOWS

2.1. Introduction and Objectives

This lesson introduces commands and basic tools for both Windows and Linux operating systems so that you can become familiar with them. These commands will be used to complete the exercises in the following lessons

At the end of this lesson, you should know the following commands:

1. General Windows and Linux commands
2. Basic network commands and tools

- ping
- tracert
- netstat
- ipconfig
- route

2.2. Requirements and Setup

2.2.1 Requirements

For the lesson,

the following are needed:

- a PC with Windows 98/Me/2000/NT/XP/2003
- a PC with Linux Suse/Debian/Knoppix
- access to the Internet.

2.2.2 Setup

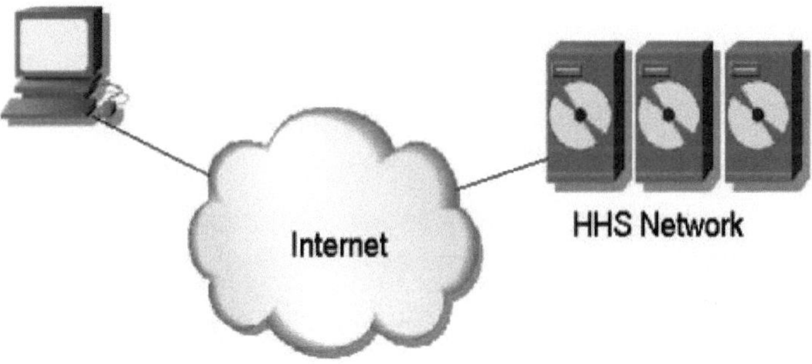

This is the setup in which you are going to work. It consists of your PC, with access to the Internet, and the ISECOM Hacker Highschool network, which you will access through the Internet. This is the network against which you will make most of the tests.

Note that access to the ISECOM test network is restricted. In order to gain access to it, your instructor must contact the sytem administrator.

2.3. System Operation: WINDOWS

Most of the tools used for the study of networks are internal commands in the Windows operating system. Therefore, we are going to explain how to open a command window when the Windows operating system is being used.

2.3.1 How to open an MS-DOS window

To issue the following commands, it is necessary to open a command prompt (an MS-DOS window). The procedure for this is the same for all versions of Windows.

1.- Click the START button

2.- Choose the RUN option

3.- Type "command" if you are using Windows 95/98 or "cmd" for all other versions of Windows and press Enter or click OK.

4.- A window similar to the following one will appear:

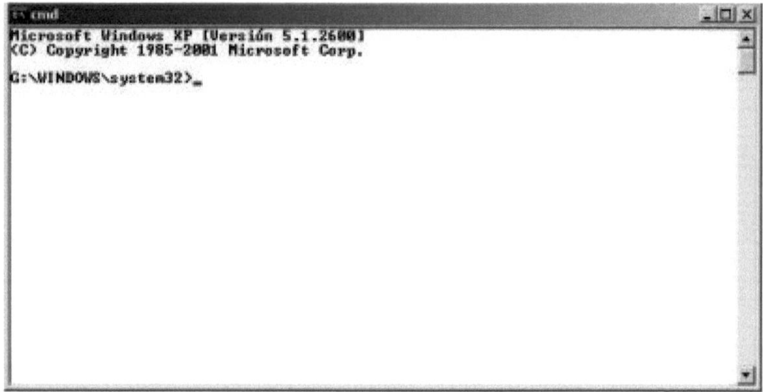

5.- Now the commands and tools listed below can be entered.

2.3.2 Commands and tools (Windows)

2.3.2 Commands and tools (Windows)

Commands

date	Display or set the date of the system
time	Display or set the time of the system
ver	Display the MS-DOS version that is being used
dir	Display the list of subdirectories and files of a directory
cls	Clear the screen
mkdir, **md *directory***	Make a directory with the name "directory" Example: md tools
chdir, cd *directory*	Display the name or change the current directory to "directory" Example: cd tools
rmdir, rd *directory*	Delete the directory with the name "directory" Example: rd tools
tree *directory*	Display the structure of folders of a path in text-graphic format Example: tree c:\tools
chkdsk	Check a disk and show a status report
mem	Show the amount of memory used and free in the system
rename, **ren *source dest***	Change the name of files Example: ren oldname newname
copy *source dest*	Copy one or more files to another location Example: copy c:\tools\myfile.txt c:\tmp
move *source dest*	Move files and change the name of files and directories Example: move c:\tools c:\tmp
type *file*	Type the content of one or more text files Example: type c:\tools\myfile.txt
more *file*	Display the information screen by screen Example: more c:\tools\myfile.txt
delete, del *file*	Delete one or more files Example: del c:\tools\myfile.txt

Note: The words in italics are not commands, and must be replaced by the desired values. Some of the commands can be used by typing either their long version or short version; for example, "delete" and "del," are the same command.

Tools

ping *host*	Verify contact with the machine "host" The command ping sends "packets" using ICMP (Internet Control Message Protocol) to another computer, to learn whether it is accessible through the network. In addition, it shows a statistical summary about the percentage of packets that have not been answered and the response time. The name of the machine can be used directly or its IP address. Examples: ping www.google.com ping 193.145.85.2 Some options are: - n N: send N packets - t: ping the specified host until stopped (press CTRL+C to end) To see more options: ping /h

tracert *host*	Show the route that packets follow to reach the machine "host" The command tracert is the abbreviation of trace route, which allows you to learn the route that a packet follows from the origin, (your machine) to the destination machine. It can also tell you the time it takes to make each jump. At the most, 30 jumps will be listed. It is sometimes interesting to observe the names of the machines through which the packets travel. Examples: tracert www.google.com tracert 193.145.85.2 Some options are: - h N: to specify N, at the most, jumps. - d: to not show the names of the machines. To see more options: tracert
ipconfig	Display information on the active interfaces (ethernet, ppp, etc.) in the computer. Some options: /all: to show more details /renew *name*: renews connection with "name" when automatic configuration with DHCP is used. /release *name*: deactivates all matching connections when automatic configuration with DHCP is used. To see more options: ipconfig /?
route print	Display the routing table The command route serves to define static routes, to erase routes or simply to see the state of the routes.

	Some options: print: to show the list of routes. delete: to delete a route. add: to add a route. To see more options: route/?
netstat	Displays information on the status of the network and established connections with remote machines. Some options: -a: To sample all the connections and listening ports -n: to display addresses and port numbers in numeric form -e: to sample Ethernet statistics For example: netstat - an To see more options: netstat/?

For additional information on these commands and tools type "command /h" or "command /?," or "help command" from a MS-DOS window.

For example, for additional information on the tool netstat, we have three possibilities:

1) netstat /h
2) netstat /?
3) help netstat

2.4. System Operations:

Linux Just as in Windows, if you are using Linux, a great majority of the commands that you will use are executed from a console emulation window. Therefore, we will next learn how to open a console window in Linux.

2.4.1 How to open a console window

To issue the following commands, it is necessary to open a console window:

1. - To go to the START APPLICATION button

2. - Select "Run Command"
3. - Enter "konsole"
4. - A window similar to the following one will appear:

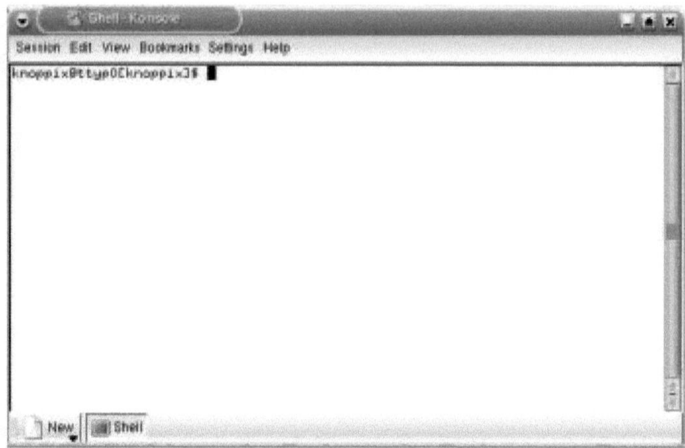

5. - Now the commands and tools listed below can be entered.

2.4.2 Commands and tools (Linux)

pwd	Display the name of the current directory.
hostname	Display the name of the local host (the computer which you are currently using)

finger user	Display information on the user "user" Example: finger root
ls	List the content of the directories Example: ls -la
cd directory	Change from current directory to "directory". If no directory name is specified it changes to the home directory. Example: For the login name "mylogin" the command $cd changes the directory to /home/mylogin Example: $cd - changes to the last visited directory Example: $cd /tmp changes to the "tmp" directory
cp source dest	Copy files. Copy the file "source" to the file "dest". Example: cp /etc/passwd /tmp
rm file	Delete files. Only the owner of the file (or root) can delete it. Example: rm myfile
mv source dest	Move or rename files and directories. Example: mv oldname newname
mkdir directory	Make a directory with the name "directory". Example: mkdir tools
rmdir directory	Delete the directory with the name "directory" if it is empty. Example: rmdir tools
find / -name file	Find a file with the name "file" beginning the search in the root directory Example: find / -name myfile
echo string	Write the string "string" in the standard output Example: echo hello
command > file	Redirect the normal screen output of the command "command" to the file "file" Example: ls > myls
command >> file	Redirect the normal screen output of the command "command" to the file "file". If the file already exists, it appends the output to the end of the file. Example: ls >> myls
man command	Show the pages of the online manual about "command" Example: man ls

For additional information on the use of these commands and tools, type in "command -help" or "man command" in the console window.

For example, for additional information on the "ls" command, type in either of these two possibilities:

1) ls —help

2) man ls

Tools (Please see the Windows section for details on these tools.)

ping *host*	Verify the contact with the machine "host" Example: ping www.google.com
traceroute *host*	Show the route that the packets follow to reach the machine "host". Example: tracert www.google.com
ifconfig	Display information on the active interfaces (ethernet, ppp, etc.)
route	Display the routing table
netstat	Display information on the status of the network Example: netstat -an

Basic command equivalences for Windows/Linux

This is a table showing the basic command equivalences between Linux and Windows. Commands are executed from a shell (in Linux) or from a MS-DOS window (in Windows).

Linux	Windows
command --help	command /h, command /?
man command	help command
cp	copy
rm	del
mv	move
mv	ren
more, less, cat	type
lpr	print
rm -R	deltree
ls	dir
cd	cd
mkdir	md
rmdir	rd
route	route print
traceroute –I	tracert
ping	ping
ifconfig	ipconfig

2.5. Exercises

2.5.1 Exercises in Windows

1. Go to a MS-DOS window.

2. Identify the version of MS-DOS that you are using. What version have you detected? What command have you used?.

3. Identify the date and time of the system. If they are incorrect, modify them so that they are correct. What command have you used?

4. Identify all the directories and files that are in “c:\”. What command have you used?

5. Create the directory c:\hhs\lesson0. Copy in this directory all the files with the extension “.sys” that are in “c:\”. What files have you found? What commands have you used?

6. Identify the IP address of your host. What command have you used? What IP address do you have?

7. Trace the route to “www.google.com”. Identify IPs of the intermediate routers.

2.5.2 Exercises in Linux

1. Identify the owner of the file “passwd”. (Note: first locate where this file is). What command have you used?

2. Create the directory “work” in your own home directory (for example, if your login is “mylogin”, create the directory in “/home/mylogin”), and copy the file “passwd” in the directory “work” that you have just created. Identify the owner of the file “passwd” that has been copied.

3. Create the directory “.hide” in the “work” directory. List the contents of this directory. What did you have to do to see the contents of directory ".hide"?

4. Create the file “test1” with the content “This is the content of the file test1” in the “work” directory. Create the file “test2” with the

content “This is the content of the file test2” in the “work” directory. Copy into a file with the name "test” the contents of previous files. What commands have you used?

5. Identify the name and the IP address of your machine. What commands have you used? What IP address do you have?

6. Trace the route to “www.google.com”. Identify IPs of the intermediate routers.

2.5.3 Exercise 3

Complete the following table with parallelisms between Windows and Linux. For example: the Linux command “command -help” is equivalent to the Windows 13 LESSON 2 – BASIC COMMANDS IN LINUX AND WINDOWS command “command /h”. As another example, in Linux: “cp” is just like the Windows command, “copy”.

	Microsoft Windows
command --help	command /h
cp	copy
	del
mv	
more	
	print
	deltree
ls	
cd	
	md
	rd
route	
	tracert
Ping	
	ipconfig

III

PORTS AND PROTOCOLS

3.1 Introduction

The text and exercises in this lesson try to impart a basic understanding of the ports and protocols in current use, as well as their relevance within the operating systems, Windows and Linux.

The text and exercises in this lesson try to impart a basic understanding of the ports and protocols in current use, as well as their relevance within the operating systems, Windows and Linux.

At the end of the lesson you should have a basic knowledge of:

- the concepts of networks
- IP addresses
- ports and protocols

3.2 Basic concepts of networks

3.2.1 Devices

In order to understand the explanation of protocols and ports, it is necessary for you to become familiar with the icons that represent the most common devices that are seen in the basic schemes. These are:

3.2.2 Topologies

With these devices, local area networks (or LANs) can be created. In a LAN, computers can share resources, such as hard drives, printers and internet connections, and an administrator can control how these resources are shared. When a LAN is being designed, it is possible to choose any of the following physical topologies:

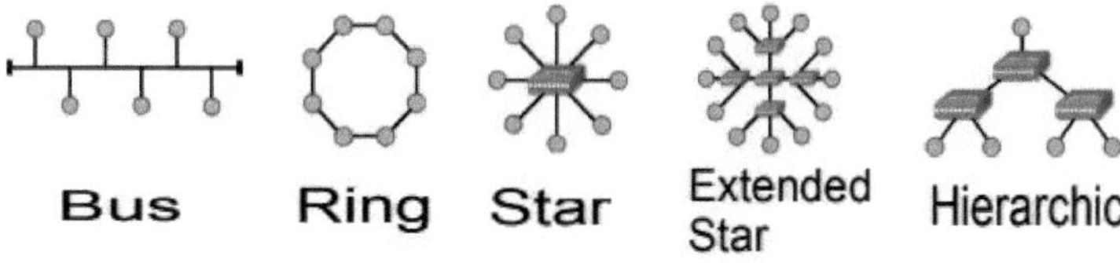

In a bus topology, all the computers are connected to a single means of transmission, and each computer can communicate directly with any of the others. In the ring configuration, each computer is connected to the following one, and the last one to the first, and each computer can only communicate directly with the two adjacent computers. In the star topology, none of the computers are directly connected with others. Instead they are connected through a central point and the device at that central point is responsible for relaying information from computer to computer. If several central points are connected to each other, an extended star topology is obtained. In a star or extended star topology, all the central points are peers, that is, each exchanges information on an equal basis. However, if you connect two star or extended star networks together using a central point which controls or limits the exchange of information between the two networks, then you have created a single, hierarchical network topology.

3.3 TCP/IP model

3.3.1 Introduction

TCP/IP was developed by the DoD (Department of Defense) of the United States and DARPA (Defense Advanced Research Project Agency) in the 1970s. TCP/IP was designed to be an open standard that anyone could use to connect computers together and exchange information between them. Ultimately, it became the basis for the Internet.

3.3.2 Layers

The TCP/IP model defines four totally independent layers into which it divides the process of communication between two devices. The layers through which it passes information between two devices are:

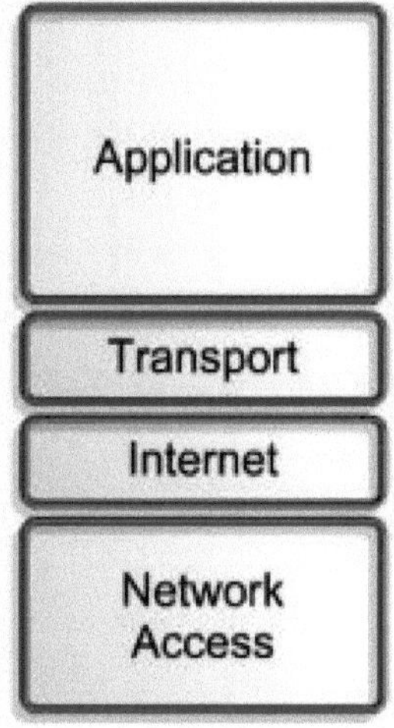

3.3.2.1 Applicatio

The application layer is the layer nearest the end user. This is the layer that is in charge of translating data from applications into information that can be sent through the network.

The basic functions of this layer are:

- Representation
- Codification
- Dialog Control
- Application Management

3.3.2.2 Transport

The transport layer establishes, maintains and finishes virtual circuits for information transfer. It provides control mechanisms for data flow and allows broadcasting, and it provides mechanisms for the detection and correction of errors. The information that arrives at this layer from the application layer is divided into different segments. Information that comes to the transport layer from the internet layer is delivered back to the application layer through ports. (See Section 3.3.5 Ports for details on ports.)

The basic functions of this layer are:

- Reliability
- Flow Control
- Error Correction
- Broadcasting

3.3.2.3 Internet

This layer divides the segments of the transport layer into packets and sends the packets across the networks that make up the Internet. It uses IP, or internet protocol addresses to determine the location of the recipient device. It does not ensure reliability in the connections, because this is already taken care of by the transport layer, but it is responsible for selecting the best route between the originating device and the recipient device.

3.3.2.4 Network Access

This layer is in charge of sending information at both the LAN level and the physical level. It transforms all the information that arrives from the superior layers into basic information (bits) and directs it to the proper location. At this level, the destination of the information is determined by the MAC, or media access control, address of the recipient device.

3.3.3 Protocols

To be able to send information between two devices, both must speak the same language. This language is called the protocol.

The protocols that appear in the application layer of the TCP/IP model are:

- File Transfer Protocol (FTP)
- Hypertext Transfer Protocol (HTTP)
- Simple Mail Transfer Protocol (smtp)
- Domain Name Service (DNS)
- Trivial File Transfer Protocol (TFTP)

The protocols of the transport layer are:

- Transport Control Protocol (TCP)
- User Datagram Protocol (UDP)

The protocols of the internet layer are:

- Internet Protocol (IP)

The protocol most often used in the network access layer is:

- Ethernet

The protocols listed above and their associated ports will be described in the following sections.

3.3.3.1 Application layer protocols

FTP or file transfer protocol is used for the transmission of files between two devices. It uses TCP to create a virtual connection for the control of information, then creates another connection to be used for the delivery of data. The most commonly used ports are 20 and 21.

HTTP or hypertext transfer protocol is used to translate information into web pages. This information is distributed in a manner similar to that used for electronic mail. The most commonly used port is 80.

SMTP or simple mail transfer protocol is a mail service that is based on the FTP model. It transfers electronic mail between two systems and provides notifications of incoming mail. The most commonly used port is 25.

DNS or domain name service provides a means to associate a domain name with an ip address. The most commonly used port is 53.

TFTP or trivial file transfer protocol has the same functions as FTP but uses UDP instead of TCP. (See Section 3.3.3.2 for details on the differences between UDP and TCP.) This gives it more speed, but less security and trustworthiness. The most commonly used port is 69.

3.3.3.2 Transport layer Protocols

There are two protocols which can be used by the transport layer to deliver information segments.

TCP or transmission control protocol establishes a logical connection between the final points of the network. It synchronizes and regulates the traffic with what is known as the "Three Way Handshake". In the "Three Way Handshake," the originating device sends an initial packet called a SYN to the recipient device. The recipient device sends an acknowledgment packet, called a SYN/ACK. The originating device then sends a packet called an ACK, which is an acknowledgment of the acknowledgment. At this point, both the originating device and the recipient device have established that there is a connection between the two and both are ready to send and receive data to and from each other.

UDP or user datagram protocol is a transport protocol which is not based on a connection. In this case, the originating device sends packets without warning the recipient device to expect these packets. It is then up to the recipient device to determine whether or not those packets will be accepted. As a result, UDP is faster that TCP, but it cannot guarantee that a packet will be accepted.

3.3.3.3 Internet layer Protocols

IP or internet protocol serves as a universal protocol to allow any two computers to communicate through any network at any time. Like UDP, it is connectionless, because it does not establish a connection with the remote computer. Instead, it is what is known as a best effort service, in that it will do whatever is possible to ensure that it works correctly, but its reliability is not guaranteed. The Internet Protocol determines the format for the packet headers, including the IP addresses of both the originating and the recipient devices.

3.3.4 IP Addresses

A domain name is the web address that you normally type into a web browser. That name identifies one or more IP addresses. For example, the domain name microsoft.com represents about a dozen IP addresses. Domain names are used in URLs to identify particular Web pages. 9 LESSON 3 – PORTS AND PROTOCOLS For example, in the URL http://www.pcwebopedia.com/index.html, the domain name is pcwebopedia.com.

Every domain name has a suffix that indicates which top level domain (TLD) it belongs to. There are only a limited number of such domains. For example:

- .gov - Government agencies
- .edu - Educational institutions
- .org - Organizations (nonprofit)
- .com - Commercial Business .net - Network organizations

Because the Internet is based on IP addresses, not domain names, every Web server requires a Domain Name System (DNS) server to translate domain names into IP addresses.

IP Addresses are the identifiers that are used to differentiate between computers and other devices that are connected to a network. Each device must have a different IP address, so that there are no problems of mistaken identity within the network. IP addresses consist of 32 bits that are divided in four 8 bit octets which are separated by dots. Part of the IP address identifies the network, and the remainder of the IP address identifies the individual computers on the network.

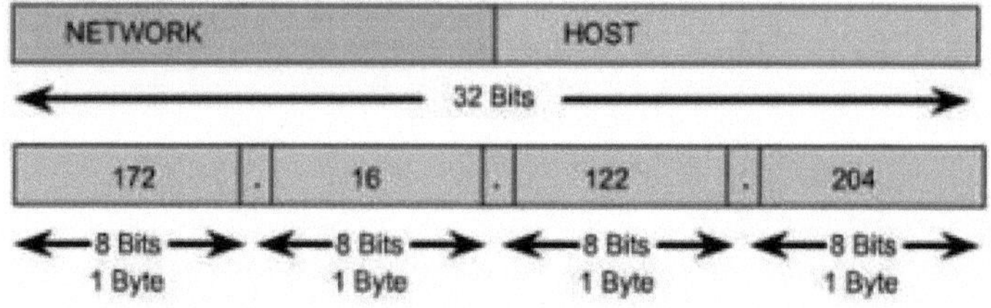

There are both public and private IP addresses. Private IP addresses are used by private networks that have no connection with outside networks. IP addresses within a private network should not be duplicated within that network, but computers on two different – but unconnected – private networks could have duplicated IP addresses. The IP addresses that are defined by IANA, the Internet Assigned Numbers Authority, as being available for private networks are:

- 10.0.0.0 through 10.255.255.255
- 172.16.0.0 through 172.31.255.255
- 192.168.0.0. through 192.168.255.255

IP addresses are divided into classes based on what portion of the address is used to identify the network and what portion is used to identify the individual computers.

Depending on the size assigned to each part, more devices will be allowed within the network, or more networks will be allowed. The existing classes are:

Class A	Network	Host		
Octet	1	2	3	4

Class B	Network		Host	
Octet	1	2	3	4

Class C	Network			Host
Octet	1	2	3	4

Class D	Host			
Octet	1	2	3	4

- Class A: The first bit is always zero, so this class includes the addresses between 0.0.0.0 and 126.255.255.255. Note: the addresses of 127.x.x.x are reserved for the services of loopback or localhost.
- Class B: The first two bits of the first octet are '10', so this class includes the addresses between 128.0.0.0 and 191.255.255.255.
- Class C: The first three bits of the first octet are '110', so this class includes the addresses between 192.0.0.0 and 223.255.255.255.
- Class D: The first four bits of the first octet are '1110', so this class includes the addresses between 224.0.0.0 and 239.255.255.255. These addresses are reserved for group multicast implementations.

- The remaining addresses are used for experimentation or for possible future allocations.

At this time, the classes are not used to differentiate between the part of the address used to identify the network and the part used to identify the individual devices. Instead, a mask is used. In the mask, a '1' binary bit represents the part containing the network identification and a '0' binary bit represents the part that identifies the individual devices. Therefore, to identify a device, in addition to the IP address, it is necessary to specify a network mask:

- IP: 172.16.1.20
- Mask: 255.255.255.0

IP addresses 127.x.x.x are reserved to be used as loopback or local host addresses, that is, they refer directly back to the local computer. Every computer has a local host address of 127.0.0.1, therefore that address cannot be used to identify different devices. There are also other addresses that cannot be used. These are the network address and the broadcast address. The network address is an address in which the part of the address which normally identifies the device is all zeros. This address cannot be used, because it identifies a network and can never be used to identify a specific device.

- IP: 172.16.1.0
- Mask: 255.255.255.0

The broadcast address is an address in which the part of the address which normally identifies the device is all ones. This address cannot be used to identify a specific device, because it is the address that is used to send information to all of the computers that belong to the specified network.

- IP: 172.16.1.255

- Mask: 255.255.255.0

3.3.5 Ports

Both TCP and UDP use ports to exchange information with applications. A port is an extension of an address, similar to adding an apartment or room number to a street address. A letter with a street address will arrive at the correct apartment building, but without the apartment number, it will not be delivered to the correct recipient. Ports work in much the same way. A packet can be delivered to the correct IP address, but without the associated port, there is no way to determine which application should act on the packet.

Once the ports have been defined, it is possible for the different types of information that are sent to one IP address to then be sent to the appropriate applications. By using ports, a service running on a remote computer can determine what type of information a local client is requesting, can determine the protocol needed to send that information, and maintain simultaneous communication with a number of different clients.

For example, if a local computer attempts to connect to the website www.osstmm.org, whose IP address is 62.80.122.203, with a web server running on port 80, the local computer would connect to the remote computer using the socket address :

- 62.80.122.203:80

In order to maintain a level of standardization among the most commonly used ports, IANA has established that the ports numbered from 0 to 1024 are to be used for common services. The remaining ports – up through 65535 – are used for dynamic allocations or particular services.

The most commonly used ports – as assigned by the IANA – are listed here:

Port Assignments		
Decimals	**Keywords**	**Description**
0		Reserved
1-4		Unassigned
5	rje	Remote Job Entry
7	echo	Echo
9	discard	Discard
11	systat	Active Users
13	daytime	Daytime
15	netstat	Who is Up or NETSTAT
17	qotd	Quote of the Day
19	chargen	Character Generator
20	ftp-data	File Transfer [Default Data]
21	ftp	File Transfer [Control]
22	ssh	SSH Remote Login Protocol

Port Assignments		
Decimals	**Keywords**	**Description**
23	telnet	Telnet
25	smtp	Simple Mail Transfer
37	time	Time
39	rlp	Resource Location Protocol
42	nameserver	Host Name Server
43	nicname	Who Is
53	domain	Domain Name Server
67	bootps	Bootstrap Protocol Server
68	bootpc	Bootstrap Protocol Client
69	tftp	Trivial File Transfer
70	gopher	Gopher
75		any private dial out service
77		any private RJE service
79	finger	Finger
80	www-http	World Wide Web HTTP
95	supdup	SUPDUP
101	hostname	NIC Host Name Server
102	iso-tsap	ISO-TSAP Class 0
110	pop3	Post Office Protocol - Version 3
113	auth	Authentication Service
117	uucp-path	UUCP Path Service
119	nntp	Network News Transfer Protocol
123	ntp	Network Time Protocol
137	netbios-ns	NETBIOS Name Service
138	netbios-dgm	NETBIOS Datagram Service
139	netbios-ssn	NETBIOS Session Service
140-159		Unassigned
160-223		Reserved

3.3.6 Encapsulation

When a piece of information – an e-mail message, for example – is sent from one computer to another, it is subject to a series of transformations. The application layer generates the data, which is then sent to the transport layer. The transport layer takes this information and adds a header to it. This header contains information, such as the IP addresses of the originating and recipient computers, that explains what must be done to the data in order to get it to the appropriate destination. The next layer adds yet another header, and so on. This recursive procedure is known as encapsulation.

Each layer after the first makes its data an encapsulation of the previous layer's data, until you arrive at the final layer, in which the actual transmission of data occurs. The following figure explains encapsulation in a graphic form:

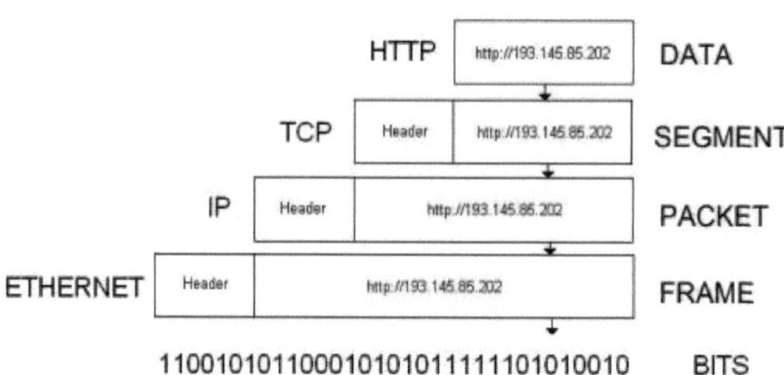

Enter Caption

When the encapsulated information arrives at its destination, it must then be de-encapsulated. As each layer receives information from the previous layer, it removes the unneeded information contained in the header placed there by the previous layer.

3.4 Exercises

3.4.1 Exercise 1: Netstat

Netstat

The Netstat command allows you to see the state of the ports on a computer. In order to execute it, you must open an MS-DOS window and type:

- netstat

In the MS-DOS window, you will then see a list of the established connections. If you want to see the connections displayed in numeric form, type:

- netstat - n

To see the connections and the active ports, type:

- netstat - an

To see a list of other options, type:

- netstat - h

In the Netstat output, the second and third columns list the local and remote IP addresses being used by the active ports. Why are the addresses of the remote ports different from the local addresses?

Next, using a web browser, open this web page:

http://193.145.85.202

then return to the MS-DOS prompt and run Netstat again. What new connection (or connections) appear? Open another web browser and go to this web page:

http://193.145.85.203 Return to the MS-DOS prompt and run Netstat:

Why does the protocol HTTP appear in several lines?

What differences exist between each one of them?

If there are several web browsers open, how does the computer know which information goes to which browser?

3.4.2 Exercise 2: Ports and Protocols

In this lesson, you learned that ports are used to differentiate between services.

Why is it that when a web browser is used, no port is specified?

What protocols are used?

Is it possible that one protocol gets used in more than one instance?

3.4.3 Exercise 3:

My First Server To perform this exercise, you must have the Netcat program. If you do not have it, you can download it from the page:

- http://www.atstake.com/research/tools/network_utilities/

Once you have Netcat installed, open an MS-DOS window. Change to the Netcat directory and type:

- nc - h

This displays the options that are available in Netcat. To create a simple server, type:

- nc - l - p 1234

When this command executes, port 1234 is opened and incoming connections are allowed. Open a second MS-DOS window and type:

- netstat – a

This should verify that there is a new service listening on port 1234. Close this MS-DOS window.

To be able to say that a server has been implemented, you must establish a client association. Open an MS-DOS window and type:

- nc localhost 1234

With this command, a connection is made with the server that is listening to port 1234. Now, anything that is written in either of the two open MS-DOS windows can be seen in the other window.

Create a file named 'test', that contains the text, "Welcome to the Hacker Highschool server!" In an MS-DOS window, type:

- nc - l - p 1234 > test

From another MS-DOS window, connect to the server by typing:

- nc localhost 1234

When the client connects to the server, you should see the output of the file, 'test'. To close the service, switch to the MS-DOS window in which it is running and press CTRL-C.

What protocol has been used to connect with the server?

Does Netcat allow you to change this? If so, how?

IV

SERVICES AND CONNECTIONS

4.0 Introduction

The purpose of this lesson is to give you an understanding of some of the basic services which networks use to provide and exchange information, and to discuss some of the methods in which personal computers and local networks connect with the other networks which make up the Internet.

4.1 Services

You have a computer, and you know that there is useful information on this computer, but not very much. You also know that other people, millions of other people also have computers, and that their computers will also have useful information.

Now, you can assume that these other people, and these other computers may very likely have lots of information on them that would be of interest to you. The only problem is how to access all this useful information that may be on other people's computers.

The computers themselves can communicate with each other, easily, through ports, using the different protocols that have been designed, but that doesn't really help you. You can't understand the streams of binary data that the computers exchange between themselves. You need some way for your computer to interpret the information that it can receive from the other computers in some way that you can use it.

The programs that the computers use to translate the data that they exchange into a form that is useful to you are call services. These services allow you to view web pages, exchange e-mail, chat, and interact in remote computers in many other different ways.

Your computer, the local computer uses programs called clients to interpret the information that you receive. The other computers, the remote computers, use programs called servers to provide this information to your computer.

4.1.1 HTTP and The Web

When you say, 'the Internet,' what comes to mind for most people is, in fact, the World Wide Web. The World Wide Web, or just the Web, is not the Internet. Instead, it is a method of using the Internet to exchange information between computers. The Web uses http or hypertext transfer protocol and services known as web browsers and web servers to allow information in the form of web pages to be exchanged between local and remote computers.

On the local side, what you see is the web browser. Information from the remote computer is sent to your local computer using the http protocol. The web browser interprets that information and displays it on your local computer in the form of web pages.

The *hypertext* part of the http protocol refers to a non-linear method of presenting information. Text is normally read in a linear fashion: word 2 follows word 1; sentence 3 follows sentence 2; paragraph 5 follows paragraph 4. The idea of hypertext allows information to be viewed in a non-linear way. This is the major difference between hypertext and the older, plain text methods of displaying information.

With *hypertext*, words and ideas can connect, not only with the words that directly surround them, but also with other words, ideas or images. Hypertext is not restricted to the Web. Most full-featured word processors will allow you to create locally stored pages in web or http format. These pages are read using your web browser and act as would any other web page, only they are stored on your local computer, not a remote computer.

On your local computer, you use a client program called a web browser. Contrary to what you might have been lead to believe, there are actually a number of web browsers available for both Windows and Linux. These include Microsoft's Internet Explorer, Netscape Navigator, and the Mozilla Firefox browsers.

You can also create your own web page. The easiest way to do this is to use one of the common word processors, such as OpenOffice, Microsoft Word, or WordPerfect. These programs will allow you to produce simple web pages, combining text, hypertext and images.

Plenty of people have made useful, clever and innovative web pages using these simple tools. But these pages aren't flashy. Flashy means frames and scripts and animations.

It also means spending lots of money on a fancy web page design program. These programs allow you to create many interesting effects on your web page, but they are more complex to use than the word processors that you are probably already familiar with.

Once you have the pages designed, you'll need a computer to put them on, so that other people can view them. This is called web hosting. The hosting computer will be running a web server. It is possible to run one of these servers from your own home, using your own computer, but there are several drawbacks, the primary one of these being persistence. Information stored on a web server is only available when that server is powered up, operating properly and has an open connection.

So, if you want to run a web server from your own bedroom, you have to leave your computer on all the time; you have to make sure that the web server program is operating properly all the time (this includes troubleshooting hardware problems, controlling viruses, worms and other attacks, and dealing with the inevitable bugs and flaws within the program itself), and you have to keep a connection to the Internet open.

This is why most people pay someone else to do all this. A web hosting company will store your web page on their computer. A perfect web hosting company will have multiple, redundant servers and a regular backup policy, so that your service is not lost because of hardware problems, a support staff to keep the server running despite hacker attacks and program bugs, and a number of open connections to the Internet, so that all your have to do is design your web page, upload it to the hosting company's server, hang up the phone, turn off the computer, and go to sleep, and your web page will be available to the entire world.

It's also possible to find organizations that offer free web hosting. Some of these organizations are funded by paid advertising, which means that anyone who wants to view your web page will first have to view someone else's advertisement. But they don't have to buy anything, and you don't have to pay anything.

4.1.2 E-Mail – POP and SMTP

The second most visible aspect of the Internet is probably e-mail. On your computer, you use an e-mail client, which connects to a mail server. When you set up your e-mail account, you are given a unique name in the form of user@domain. You are also asked to provide a password to use to retrieve your e-mail. The SMTP protocol, which is used to send e-mail, does not require a password.

This may not have been a fault when the protocol was designed, and the Internet was a small world inhabited by like minded people, but now it has become a loophole which allows for unauthorized use of mail servers and various other tricks, such as 'e-mail spoofing', in which someone sends an e-mail that appears to come from another address.

However, some mail servers minimize this flaw by implementing an authentication step, in which you must prove your identity before you can send an e-mail.

One important thing to remember is, despite being password protected, e-mail is not a way to send secure information. Most POP clients and servers require that your password be communicated – unencrypted – to your mail server. This doesn't mean than anyone who receives an e-mail from you also receives your password; but it does mean that someone with the right knowledge and tools can relatively easily 'sniff out' your password. (For ideas on making your e-mail more secure, see Lesson 9: E-mail Security.)

4.1.3 IRC

IRC, or Internet relay chat, is where the unregulated nature of the Internet is most clearly expressed. On IRC, anyone with anything to say gets a chance to say it.

You may be familiar with the chat rooms used by certain online services. IRC is just like a chat room, only there are no rules, there are no standards, and – quite often – there are no chaperones.

You may find exactly what you are looking for on an IRC channel, or you just may find something that you had rather you never knew existed. All the rules that you've heard about chat rooms are applicable to IRC channels. Don't tell anyone your real name. Don't give out your phone number, your address, or your bank account numbers. But have fun!

Exercises:

Find and join three IRC channels which focus on security topics. How do you join in the public conversation? What do you have to do to have a private conversation with a person?

It is possible to exchange files through IRC. How could you do this? Would you always want to exchange files through IRC? Why or why not?

4.1.4 FTP

FTP stands for file transfer protocol. As the name implies, it allows for files to be transferred between a local and a remote computer. While it can be used for private file transfers, it is more commonly associated with free, anonymous ftp servers which offer public access to collections of files. Anonymous ftp was once the means by which most computer users exchanged files over the Internet.

While many anonymous ftp servers are used to distribute files that are available illegally(and are possibly infected with viruses), there are also many which are legally used to distribute programs and files. Servers which offer anonymous ftp services can be found through various means, including Internet search engines.

Most anonymous ftp servers now allow you to access their files using the ftp protocol through a web browser.

Exercises:

Both Windows and Linux come with a basic, command line ftp client; to access it, open a command prompt or terminal window and type:

```
ftp
```

At the `ftp>` prompt, you can type `help`, to get a list of available commands.

```
ftp> help
Commands may be abbreviated.  Commands are:
!          delete      literal    prompt    send
?          debug       ls         put       status
append     dir         mdelete    pwd       trace
ascii      disconnect  mdir       quit      type
```

```
bell      get    mget   quote       user
binary    glob   mkdir  recv        verbose
bye       hash   mls    remotehelp
cd        help   mput   rename
close     lcd    open   rmdir
```

Some important commands are:

- ftp> open

Which connects you to the ftp server named domain.name.

- ftp> ls

or

- ftp> dir

Which lists the contents of the remote working directory.

- ftp> cd

Which changes the remote working directory to a directory named newdir.

- ftp> get

Which downloads a file named filename from the remote computer to the local computer.

- ftp> mget

Which downloads files named file1, file2, and file3 from the remote computer to the local computer.

- ftp> close

Which disconnects you from the remote ftp server.

- ftp> quit

Which shuts down your local ftp client.

To connect to an anonymous ftp service, you must first open your local ftp client:

- ftp

Use the open command to connect to the server. The command

- ftp> open

connects your ftp client with the anonymous ftp server named anon.server. When the remote ftp server makes its connection, it will identify itself to your local client, then ask for a user name. Connected to anon.server. 220 ProFTPD Server (Welcome . . .) User (anon.server:(none)): For most anonymous ftp servers,

you should enter in the word anonymous as the user name. The remote ftp server will acknowledge that you are connecting as an anonymous user, and will give you instructions on what to use as a password. 331 Anonymous login ok, send your complete email address as your password.

n most cases, the remote server does not check the validity of the email address entered as a password, so it will not stop you from accessing the server if you enter an invalid address. However, this is considered to be a breach of etiquette. After you have entered a password, the remote server will send a welcome message to your local computer.

230-

- Welcome to ftp.anon.server, the public ftp server of anon.server. We hope you find what you're looking for.
- If you have any problems or questions, please send email to ftpadmin@anon.server

230 Anonymous access granted, restrictions apply.

From here, you can use the ls, dir, cd and get commands to download files from the remote server to your local computer.

Using these examples, see if you can download a file from an anonymous ftp server. Use your web browser and a search engine to find an anonymous ftp server which has a copy of Alice in Wonderland, then, using the command line ftp client – not your web browser – try to download the file.

4.1.5 Telnet and SSH

Telnet allows a local user to send a wide variety of commands to a remote computer. This allows the local user to instruct the remote computer to perform functions and return data to the local computer, almost as if you were sitting at a keyboard in front of the remote computer. SSH, or secure shell is intended as a secure replacement for telnet.

Again, both Windows and Linux come with a basic, command line telnet client; to access it, open a command prompt or terminal window and type: telnet.

To access a telnet server, you will need to have an account and password set up for you by the administrator of the server, because the telnet program allows you to perform a large number of actions, some of which could severely compromise the remote computer.

Telnet was used in the past to allow computer administrators to remotely control servers and to provide user support from a distance. Telnet can also be used for a number of other tasks, such as sending and receiving email and viewing the source code for web pages (although telnet does fall under the heading of the most difficult way to do these things). Telnet can be used to do many things that are illegal and immoral, but there are also legitimate reasons for using it.

You can use telnet to check your email, and view, not just the subject line, but the first few lines of an email, which will allow you to decide whether or not to delete the email without downloading the entire message.

4.1.6 DNS

When you want to call a friend on the phone, you need to know the correct phone number; when you want to connect to a remote computer, you also need to know its number.

You may remember from previous lessons that, for computers on the Internet, this number is called the IP address. As numbers, these IP addresses are very easily managed by computers, but as humans, we prefer to use what are called domain names. For example, to connect to the Hacker web page, we type '**www.kunalmaurya.com**' into the address bar of a web browser. However, the web browser can't use this name to connect to the server that hosts the Hacker web page – it must use the IP address.

This means that your local computer must have some means of translating domain names into IP addresses. If there were only hundreds, or even thousands of computers on the Internet, then it might be possible for you to have a simple table stored on your computer to use to look up these addresses, but, not only are there are millions of computers on the Internet, the correlations between domain names and IP addresses can change daily.

For this reason, DNS or Domain Name Service is used to translate domain names into IP addresses. When you type the domain name www.domainname.com into your web browser, your web browser contacts the DNS server chosen by your ISP. If that DNS server has www.domainname.com in its database, then it will return the IP address to your computer, allowing you to connect.

If your DNS server doesn't have www.domainname.com in its database, then it will send a request to another DNS server, and it will keep sending requests to other DNS servers until it finds the correct IP address, or it establishes that the domain name is invalid.

Exercises:

To learn more about DNS:

Open an MS-DOS window and identify the IP address of your computer. What command have you used? What IP address do you have?

Identify the IP address of your DNS server.

What command have you used?

What is the IP address of the DNS server. Ping www.isecom.org. Do you receive an affirmative answer? What IP address answers the ping?

Can you direct your computer to use a different DNS server? If so, change the configuration of your computer so that it uses a different DNS server.

Ping www.isecom.org again. Do you receive the same response? Why?

4.1.7 DHCP

DHCP or Dynamic Host configuration Protocol allows for IP addresses to be dynamically allocated within a network. The network is given a block of IP addresses for its use.

When a computer joins the network, it is assigned an IP address. When a computer leaves, its IP address becomes available for use by another computer. This is useful for large networks of computers, since it is not necessary for each computer to have an individually assigned, static IP address. Instead, you use a DHCP server. When a new computer connects to the network, the first thing that it does is request an IP address from the DHCP server. Once it has been assigned an IP address, the computer then has access to all the services of the network.

4.2 Connections

Most computers connect to the Internet through a modem. Modems translate the digital signals produced by computers into analog signals that can be transmitted across commonly available telephone lines. Modem speeds are measured in baud or bits per second. Higher baud rates are better, since they allow for faster transmission of data, but you must also consider what you are planning to do. There are certain applications – such as telnetting into MUDs – for which a twenty year old 300 baud modem would still be acceptable (provided your typing speed wasn't so good), while high bandwidth applications such as streaming video can often strain even the most powerful cable modems.

4.2.1 ISPs

You don't just call up the Internet. You need to access a server that will connect your computer to the Internet. The server does all the heavy work, like being on all the time. The server is run by an ISP or Internet Service Provider. An ISP has a point-of-presence on the Internet that is constant, and it has servers that run the services you are going to use. Now, you can run these services on your own. For example, you can run a mail server on your local computer, but it will require you to have your computer powered up and connected to a network all the time, just waiting for those brief moments when information has to be exchanged. An ISP, however, consolidates the efforts of a large number of users, so the mail server is working all the time, instead of sitting around, doing nothing. Additionally, an ISP's computers are going to use a high speed connection to connect to a NAP or Network Access Point. These NAPs then interconnect with each other through ultra-high speed connections called backbones. This is the Internet.

4.2.2 Plain Old Telephone Service

POTS, or plain old telephone service, is still the most widely used method of accessing the Internet. Its primary disadvantage is its low speed, but in many cases this is made up for by its wide availability. Most national Internet service providers have a large number of local access numbers, and almost everyone still has a phone with a land line. In theory, if you had an acoustic modem and a pocket full of change, you could connect from almost any public pay phone. Not that you would really want to do that. POTS is slow. The fastest telephone modems are rated at a speed of 56,600 baud. That, however, as they explain in the small print, is a lie. Power constraints limit the actual download speed to about 53,000 baud and the effective rate is usually much lower. This doesn't compare very well with DSL or cable modems. That said, telephone service is widely available, and POTS based ISPs are relatively cheap (and sometimes free). You wouldn't want to trade pirated movies over POTS, because it's immoral, illegal and ties up your phone line all night and maybe into the afternoon, but you could certainly send friendly, text based e-mails to Granny. And if you used telnet, you could even do it with a dusty DOS based machine that you pulled out of the basement.

4.2.3 DSL

DSL or digital subscriber line, is a method of sending large amounts of information over the wires that already exist for the POTS. Its main advantage over POTS is that it is much faster than analog modems, and it provides a permanent connection. In addition, it allows you to make and receive regular telephone calls while you are connected to the Internet. Its main disadvantage is that its availability is limited by your proximity to the telephone company's switching equipment – if you live too far down the line; you're out of luck.

4.2.4 Cable Modems

Cable modems do not use the traditional telephone lines to connect to the Internet. Instead they make use of the optical fiber lines that are used by cable companies to transmit digital cable signals. Like DSL, cable modems allow you to make and receive regular telephone calls while you are connected to the Internet, and they provide a permanent connection, but cable modems are generally faster than DSL. Cable modems have two basic flaws. The first is that cable modem access is a shared resource, so your connection speeds will be decreased when there are other users in close geographic proximity. The second is that cable modem access is only available in areas where cable companies have installed the necessary fiber optic wiring.

V

SYSTEM IDENTIFICATION

5.0 Introduction

It is obvious that someone who sits down at the keyboard of your computer can gather information about it, including the operating system and the programs that are running, but it is also possible for someone to use a network connection to gather information about a remote computer. This lesson will describe some of the ways in which that information can be gathered. Knowing how this information is gathered will help you to ensure that your local computer is safe from these activities.

5.1 Identifying a Server

There are a number of useful sources on the Web which will allow you to collect information about domain names and IP addresses.

5.1.1 Identifying the Owner of a Domain

The first step in identifying a remote system is to look at the domain name or IP address. Using a Whois lookup, you can discover valuable information, including the identity of the owner of a domain and contact information, which may include addresses and phone numbers. Note that there are now a number of domain name registrars, and not all whois databases contain information for all domains. You may have to look at more that one whois database to find information on the domain that you are investigating.

5.1.2 Identifying the IP address of a Domain

There are a number of ways to determine the IP address of a domain. The address may be contained in the whois information or you may have to use a DNS or Domain Name Service lookup. (A web search engine will provide a number of resources for discovering IP addresses from domain names.)

Once you have the IP address, you can access the records of the various members of the Number Resource Organization (http://www.arin.net/ or http://www.ripe.net/), to gain information about how IP addresses are distributed. IP numbers are assigned to service providers and networks in large groups, and knowing which group an IP address is contained in, and who has the rights to that group, can be very useful. This can help you determine information about the server or service provider that a website uses.

Exercises:

Pick a valid domain name and use a Whois lookup to find out who owns that domain. dominio (http://www.whois.com -> "isecom.org"+Go -> Whois Lookup) What other information is available? When was the domain created? When will it expire? When was it last updated? Find the IP address for this domain name.

Using the whois lookups for the various members of the Number Resource Organization determine who this IP address has been assigned to. (Start with the www.arin.net, page, which also links to the other members of the NRO.) What is the range of the other numbers that have also been registered to this entity?

5.2 Identifying Services

Once you have established the owner and the IP address of a domain, then you can start to look for information about the server to which that domain refers.

5.2.1 Ping and TraceRoute

Now that you know who owns the domain, and who the IP number has been assigned to, you can check to see if the server that the website is on is actually active. The ping command will tell you if there is actually a computer associated with that domain or IP. The command

- ping domain
- ping ipaddress

will tell you if there is an active computer at that address.

If the output of the ping command indicates that the packets sent were received, then you can assume that the server is active.

Another command, tracert (in Windows) or traceroute (in Linux) will show you the steps that information takes as it travels from your computer to the remote computer. Tracing the route that the packets take will sometimes give you additional information about the computers in the network with the computer that is the target of your trace. For example, computers will similar IP addresses will often be part of the same network.

Exercises:

Ping a valid website or IP address (ping www.isecom.org or ping 216.92.116.13). If you get a successful response, ping the next IP address. Did this produce a successful response?

Use tracert or traceroute to trace the route from your local computer to the IP address that you used in the previous exercise. How many steps does it take? Do any of the listed computers have similar IP addresses?

5.2.2 Banner Grabbing

The next step in identifying a remote system is to try to connect using telnet and FTP. The server programs for these services display text messages called banners. A banner may state clearly and precisely what server program is running. For example, when you connect to an anonymous FTP server, you might get the following message:

- Connected to anon.server.
- 220 ProFTPD Server (Welcome . . .)
- User (anon.server:(none)):

While the number 220 is an FTP code which indicates that the server is ready for a new user, the text message ProFTPD Server identifies the FTP server program that is running on the remote computer. Using a web search engine, you can learn what operating system the program runs on and other details about its requirements, capabilities, limitations, and flaws. \

The primary flaw in the use of banner grabbing to gather information about a system is that clever system administrators can spoof banners. A banner that reads NoneOfYourBusiness Server is obviously misleading, but a Unix system with a banner that reads WS_FTP Server (a Windows-based FTP server) is going to complicate any intelligence gathering that may be done.

5.2.3 Identifying Services from Ports and Protocols

You can also determine what programs are running on a system by looking at what ports are open and what protocols are in use.

Start by looking at your own local computer. Go to a command line or shell prompt and run the netstat program using the -a (or all) switch:

- netstat -a

The computer will display a list of open ports and some of the services that are using those ports:

- Active Connections

Proto	Local Address	Foreign Address	State
TCP	YourComputer:microsoft-ds	YourComputer:0	LISTENING
TCP	YourComputer:1025	YourComputer:0	LISTENING
TCP	YourComputer:1030	YourComputer:0	LISTENING
TCP	YourComputer:5000	YourComputer:0	LISTENING
TCP	YourComputer:netbios-ssn	YourComputer:0	LISTENING
TCP	YourComputer:1110	216.239.57.147:http	TIME_WAIT
UDP	YourComputer:microsoft-ds	*:*	
UDP	YourComputer:isakmp	*:*	
UDP	YourComputer:1027	*:*	
UDP	YourComputer:1034	*:*	
UDP	YourComputer:1036	*:*	
UDP	YourComputer:ntp	*:*	
UDP	YourComputer:netbios-ns	*:*	
UDP	YourComputer:netbios-dgm	*:*	

From this you can see many of the programs and services that are running on your local computer – many of which you don't even realize are running.

Another program, called fport, provides information similar to that which netstat does, but it also details which programs are using the open ports and protocols. (Fport is available for free download from www.foundstone.com.) Another program, called nmap (for network mapper), will more thoroughly probe your computer for open ports.

When nmap is run, it will display a list of open ports and the services or protocols that use those ports. It may also be able to determine what operating system your computer is using. For example, if you run nmap on your local computer, you might see the following output:

```
Port   State Service
22/tcp       open   ssh
68/tcp       open   dhcpclient
139/tcp      open   netbios-ssn
445/tcp      open   microsoft-ds
Device type: general purpose
Running: Linux 2.4X|2.5.X
OS details: Linux Kernel 2.4.0 - 2.5.20
Uptime 1.024 days (since Sat Jul 4 12:15:48 2004)
```

5.3 System Fingerprinting

Now that you know how to identify a server and how to scan for open ports and use this information to determine what services are running, you can put this information together to fingerprint a remote system, establishing the most likely operating system and services that the remote computer is running.

5.3.1 Scanning Remote Computers

Using an IP address or a domain name other than 127.0.0.1 as an argument for nmap allows you to scan for open ports on remote computers. It doesn't mean that there will be open ports, or that you will find them, but it does allow you to try. For example, imagine that you have been receiving a large amount of spam e-mails, and you want to discover information about the person who is sending you these e-mails. Looking at the headers of one of the e-mails, you see that many of the e-mails have originated from the same IP address: 256.92.116.13 (see Lesson 9: E-mail Security for more details on reading e-mail headers). A whois lookup shows you that the address is part of a block assigned to a large ISP, but gives you no information regarding this particular IP address. If you then use nmap to scan the computer at that address, you get the following results:

VI
MALWARE

6.0 Introduction

"Malware" are programs or parts of programs that have a malicious ("Mal") or unpleasant effect on your computer security. This covers many different terms that you may have heard before, such as "Virus", "Worm" and "Trojan" and possibly a few that you haven't like "Rootkit", "Logicbomb" and "Spyware". This lesson will introduce, define and explain each of these subdivisions of malware, will give you examples, and will explain some of the countermeasures that can be put into place to restrict the problems caused by malware.

6.1 Viruses (Virii)

6.1.1 Introduction

Virus – this is the most common type of malware that people will be aware of. The reason that it is known as a virus, rather than anything else, is historical. The press ran the stories of the first computer virus at the same time as articles concerning the spread of AIDS. At the time, there were simple parallels that could be easily drawn between the two, propagation through interaction with a contaminated party, the reliance on a host and the ultimate "death" of anything infected. This resulted, and still does occasionally, in concerns that people could become "infected" with a computer virus.

6.1.2 Description

Viruses or virii are self-replicating pieces of software that, similar to a biological virus, attach themselves to another program, or, in the case of "macro viruses", to another file. The virus is only run when the program or the file is run or opened. It is this which differentiates viruses from worms. If the program or file is not accessed in any way, then the virus will not run and will not copy itself further.

There are a number of types of viruses, although, significantly, the most common form today is the macro virus, and others, such as the boot sector virus are now only found "in captivity".

6.1.2.1 Boot Sector Viruses

The boot sector virus was the first type of virus created. It hides itself in the executable code at the beginning of bootable disks. This meant that in order to infect a machine, you needed to boot from an infected floppy disk. A long time ago, (15 years or so) booting from floppy was a relatively regular occurrence, meaning that such viruses were actually quite well spread by the time that people figured out what was happening. This virus (and all other types) should leave a signature which subsequent infection attempts detect, so as not to repeatedly infect the same target. It is this signature that allows other software (such as Anti-Virus-software) to detect the infection.

6.1.2.2 The Executable File Virus

The Executable File virus attaches itself to files, such as .exe or .com files. Some viruses would specifically look for programs which were a part of the operating system, and thus were most likely to be run each time the computer was turned on, increasing their chances of successful propagation. There were a few ways of adding a virus to an executable file, some of which worked better than others. The simplest way (and the least subtle) was to overwrite the first part of the executable file with the virus code. This meant that the virus executed, but that the program would subsequently crash, leaving it quite obvious that there was an infection – especially if the file was an important system file.

6.1.2.3 The Terminate and Stay Resident (TSR) Virus

TSR is a term from DOS where an application would load itself into memory, and then remain there in the background, allowing the computer to run as normal in the foreground. The more complex of these viruses would intercept system calls that would expose them and return false results - others would attach themselves to the 'dir' command, and then infect every application in the directory that was listed – a few even stopped (or deleted) Anti-Virus software installed onto the systems.

6.1.2.4 The Polymorphic Virus

Early viruses were easy enough to detect. They had a certain signature to identify them, either within themselves as a method to prevent re-infection, or simply that they had a specific structure which it was possible to detect. Then along came the polymorphic virus. Poly – meaning multiple and morphic – meaning shape. These viruses change themselves each time they replicate, rearranging their code, changing encryption and generally making themselves look totally different. This created a huge problem, as instantly there were much smaller signatures that remained the same – some of the "better" viruses were reduced to a detection signature of a few bytes. The problem was increased with the release of a number of polymorphic kits into the virus writing community which allowed any virus to be recreated as a polymorph.

6.1.2.5 The Macro Virus

The Macro Virus makes use of the built-in ability of a number of programs to execute code. Programs such as Word and Excel have limited, but very powerful, versions of the Visual Basic programming language. This allows for the automation of repetitive tasks, and the automatic configuration of specific settings. These macro languages are misused to attach viral code to documents which will automatically copy itself on to other documents, and propagate. Although Microsoft has turned off the feature by default now on new installations, it used to be that Outlook would automatically execute certain code attached to e-mails as soon as they were read. This meant that viruses were propagating very quickly by sending themselves to all of the e-mail addresses that were stored on the infected machine.

Exercises:

1) Using the internet, try to find an example of each of the above types of virus.

2) Research the Klez virus:

- what is its "payload"
- the Klez virus is well know for SPOOFING. What is spoofing, and how does Klez use it?
- you just learned that your computer is infected with Klez. Research how to remove it.

3) You just received an email with the following Subject "Warning about your email account". The body of the message explains that your inappropriate use of email will result in your losing Internet privileges and that you should see the attachment for details. But you haven't done anything weird with email as far as you know. Are you suspicious? You should be. Research this information and determine what virus is attached to this message. (HINT: When you start thinking of breakfast – you're correct.)

6.2 Worms

6.2.1 Introduction

Worms are older than viruses. The first worm was created many years before the first virus. This worm made use of a flaw in the UNIX finger command to quickly bring down most of the Internet (which was much smaller at that time). This following section deals with worms.

6.2.2 Description

A worm is a program that, after it has been started, replicates without any need for human intervention. It will propagate from host to host, taking advantage of an unprotected service or services. It will traverse a network without the need for a user to send an infected file or e-mail. Most of the large incidents in the press recently have been worms rather than viruses.

Exercises:

1) Using the internet, see if you can find the first worm that was ever created.

2) Find out what vulnerability the Code Red and Nimda worms use to propagate.

6.3 Trojans and Spyware

6.3.1 Introduction

The first Trojan Horse was created by the Greeks several thousand years ago. (Think about the film "Troy" if you have seen it). The basic concept is that you sneak something nasty into an otherwise secure computer in the guise of something nicer. This can range from a downloaded game trailer to an e-mail promising naked pictures of your favorite celebrity. This section covers trojans and spyware.

6.3.2 Description

Trojans are pieces of malware which masquerade as something either useful or desirable in order to get you to run them. At this point they may well do something unpleasant to your computer such as install a backdoor or rootkit (see section 6.4), or - even worse - dial a premium rate phone number that will cost you money.

Spyware is software that installs itself surreptitiously, often from websites that you might visit. Once it is installed it will look for information that it considers valuable. This may be usage statistics regarding your web surfing, or it might be your credit card number. Some pieces of spyware blow their cover by rather irritatingly popping up advertisements all over your desktop.

Exercises:

1) Using the internet, find an example of a trojan and of spyware.

6.4 Rootkits and Backdoors

6.4.1 Introduction

Often when a computer has been compromised by a hacker, they will attempt to install a method to retain easy access to the machine. There are many variations on this, some of which have become quite famous – have a look on the Internet for "Back Orifice" !

6.4.2 Description

Rootkits and backdoors are pieces of malware that create methods to retain access to a machine. They could range from the simple (a program listening on a port) to the very complex (programs which will hide processes in memory, modify log files, and listen to a port). Often a backdoor will be as simple as creating an additional user in a password file which has super-user privileges, in the hope that it will be overlooked. This is because a backdoor is designed to bypass the system's normal authentication. Both the Sobig and MyDoom viruses install back doors as part of their payload.

Exercises:

1) Find on the Internet examples of rootkits and backdoors.

2) Research "Back Orifice", and compare its functionality to the commercially available offering for remote systems management from Microsoft.

6.5 Logicbombs and Timebombs

6.5.1 Introduction

Systems programmers and administrators can be quite odd people. It has been known for there to be measures on a system that will activate should certain criteria be met. For example: a program could be created that, should the administrator fail to log in for more than three weeks, would start to delete random bits of data from the disks. This occurred in a well-known case involving a programmer at a company called General Dynamics in 1992. He created a logicbomb which would delete critical data and which was set to be activated after he was gone. He expected that the company would then pay him significant amounts to come back and fix the problem. However, another programmer found the logic bomb before it went off, and the malicious programmer was convicted of a crime and fined $5,000 US dollars. The judge was merciful – the charges the man faced in court carried fines of up to $500,000 US dollars, plus jail time.

6.5.2 Description

Logicbombs and Timebombs are programs which have no replication ability and no ability to create an access method, but are applications or parts of applications that will cause damage to data should they become active. They can be stand-alone, or part of worms or viruses. Timebombs are programmed to release their payload at a certain time.

Logicbombs are programmed to release their payload when a certain event occurs. The idea behind timebombs, however, is also a useful one. Timebomb programming is used to allow you to download and try a program for a period of time – usually 30 days. At the end of the trial period, the program ceases to function, unless a registration code is provided. This is an example of non-malicious timebomb programming.

Exercises:

1) What other reasonable (and legal) uses might there be for timebomb and logicbomb coding.

2) Think about how you might detect such a program on your system.

6.6 Countermeasures

6.6.1 Introduction

There are a number of ways that you can detect, remove and prevent malware. Some of these are common sense, others are technological alternatives. The following section highlights some of these, with a brief explanation and examples.

6.6.2 Anti-Virus

Anti-Virus-software is available in many commercial and Open Source versions. These all work following the same method. They each have a database of known viruses and they will match the signatures of these against the files on the system to see if there are any infections. Often though, with modern viruses, these signatures are very small, and there can often be false positives - things that appear to be viruses that are not. Some virus scanners employ a technique known as heuristics, which means that they have a concept of what a virus "looks like" and can determine if an unknown application matches these criteria. Recently AntiVirus software has also crossed the boundary into Host Based Intrusion Detection, by keeping a list of files and checksums in order to increase the speed of scanning.

6.6.3 NIDS

Network intrusion detection is similar to AntiVirus software. It looks for a particular signature or behavior from a worm or virus. It can then either alert the user, or automatically stop the network traffic carrying the malware.

6.6.4 HIDS

Host based Intrusion Detection systems, such as Tripwire, are capable of detecting changes made to files. It is reasonable to expect that an application, once it is compiled, should not need to change, so watching various aspects of it, such as its size, last modification date and checksum, make it instantly obvious that something is wrong.

6.6.5 Firewalls

Worms propagate across the network by connecting to vulnerable services on each host. Apart from ensuring that none of these vulnerable services are running, the next best thing is to ensure that your firewall does not allow connections to these services. Many modern firewalls will provide some form of packet filtering similar to a NIDS which will rule out packets matching a certain signature. (Firewalls are discussed in more detail in section 7.1.2).

6.6.6 Sandboxes

The concept of a sandbox is simple. Your application has its own little world to play in and can't do anything to the rest of your computer. This is implemented as standard in the Java programming language, and can also be implemented through other utilities such as chroot in Linux. This restricts the damage that any malware can do to the host operating system by simply denying it the access required. Another option is to run a full machine inside a machine using a virtual machine product such as VMWare.

This isolates the virtual machine from the host operating system, only allowing access as defined by the user.

Example – http://www.vmware.com – VMWare virtual machines

Exercises:

1. Matching Game: Research each of the following and match it to the type of countermeasure that it is

1. http://www.vmware.com NIDS
2. http://www.tripwire.org Antivirus
3. http://www.snort.org Firewalls
4. http://www.checkpoint.com Sandboxes
5. http://www.sophos.com HIDS

2. Research Spybot Search and Destroy and determine what type of malware it protects your computer again.

3. Research how NIDs and HIDS works.

4. Research Firewall solutions on the net.

5. Look up "chroot" on the internet. Read about this type of "jail" or "sandbox".

VII
ATTACK ANALYSIS

7.0 Introduction

There are a lot of programs on your computer that will want to open up network connections. Some of these programs have valid reasons for connecting (your web browser won't work nearly as well without access to a network connection as it will with one), others have been written by people with motives ranging from questionable to criminal. If you want to protect your computer, you'll have to learn how to detect network access, and identify the source and intent. Not every attempt at network access is an attack, but if you don't know how to identify friend from foe, you might as well just leave your door open.

7.1 Netstat and Host Application Firewalls

To be able to identify an attack, you have to know what applications and processes normally run on your computer. Just looking at a graphical interface, whether in Windows or Linux, won't let you see what's going on underneath the surface. Netstat and a firewall can be used to help you identify which programs should be allowed to connect with the network.

7.1.1 Netstat

(netstat is also discussed in section 5.2.3) The netstat command will display the status of the network. Netstat can give you information about what ports are open and the IP addresses that are accessing them, what protocols those ports are using, the state of the port, and information about the process or program using the port.

At a command prompt enter:

netstat -aon (for Windows) or

netstat -apn (for Linux)

and netstat will produce a display similar to this:

Active Connections

Proto	Local Address	Foreign Address	State	PID
TCP	0.0.0.0:1134	0.0.0.0:0	LISTENING	3400
TCP	0.0.0.0:1243	0.0.0.0:0	LISTENING	3400
TCP	0.0.0.0:1252	0.0.0.0:0	LISTENING	2740
TCP	257.35.7.128:1243	64.257.167.99:80	ESTABLISHED	3400
TCP	257.35.7.128:1258	63.147.257.37:6667	ESTABLISHED	3838
TCP	127.0.0.1:1542	0.0.0.0:0	LISTENING	1516
TCP	127.0.0.1:1133	127.0.0.1:1134	ESTABLISHED	3400
TCP	127.0.0.1:1134	127.0.0.1:1133	ESTABLISHED	3400
TCP	127.0.0.1:1251	127.0.0.1:1252	ESTABLISHED	2740
TCP	127.0.0.1:1252	127.0.0.1:1251	ESTABLISHED	2740

Now, you need to match the numbers in the PID column with names of the processes that are running. In Windows, you should bring up the Windows Task Manager, by pressing CTL+ALT+DEL. (If it doesn't show a PID column, click on View, then Select Columns, then select PID.) In Linux, go to a command prompt and enter ps auxf to display the processor status.

In the case of our example results listed above, we find that PID 3400 belongs to our web browser and PID 2740 belongs to our email client, both of which we have knowingly executed, and both of which have valid reasons for establishing connections to the

Internet. However, PID 3838 belongs to a program named 6r1n.exe, and PID 1516 belongs to a program named buscanv.exe, neither of which we are familiar with.

However, just because you don't recognize the name of a program, that doesn't mean that it doesn't have a reason to be running on your system. The next step in this process is for us to go to an Internet search engine and try to discover what these two programs do.

In our search, we discover that buscanv.exe is required by our virus scanner and should be running. However, 6r1n.exe could be a trojan. Looking again at the display from netstat, we can see that the port associated with the 6r1n.exe program is 6667, an IRC port commonly used by trojans for remote access. At this point, we begin researching methods for removing the trojan.

7.1.2 Firewalls

Now, you could sit at your computer and run netstat over and over and over and over, keeping a constant vigil on the data moving in and out of your computer, or you could use a firewall program to do it for you.

A firewall monitors network traffic on your computer and uses a number of rules or filters to determine whether or not a program should be allowed to access the network. A firewall can filter data according to IP addresses and domain names, ports and protocols, or even transmitted data. This means that you can do things such as:

- block or allow all data coming from a specific IP address
- block or allow all data coming from a specific domain close or open specific ports
- block or allow specific protocols
- block or allow packets which contain specific data strings

You can also combine these filters to allow for careful control of the data that is allowed through the network. For example, you could:

- allow data from www.ibiblio.com through ports 20 or 21 only
- allow data from www.google.com that uses the UDP protocol
- allow data from www.yahoo.com only through port 80 and only if the packets contain the text string “I will not waste bandwidth”.

You, however, won’t need to work out all the rules on your own. You can take advantage of the firewalls ability to set these filters itself. After you first install a firewall, you will be hit with a flurry of warnings and requests for access, and you will have to determine whether or not a program will be allowed to access the network. (The firewall may also give you the option to let the firewall determine what rights programs have to access the network, but then you wouldn’t learn anything, would you?) This process is going to be similar to the one that we used to identify the programs listed by netstat. A program named iexplorer.exe is obviously Microsoft’s Internet Explorer and, if you use it as your web browser, then the firewall must allow it to access the Internet. But a program named cbox.exe could be anything. You’ve got no choice but to go to your preferred web search engine and check it out. (Of course, before you can do this, you’ve got to tell the firewall to allow your web browser to access the Internet.)

The firewall program should also give you the option to allow access to a program repeatedly, or just once. Some programs – like your web browser – should be allowed to access the network anytime, but for other programs – such as the ones that automatically check for program updates – you can learn a lot about how your computer works by having the firewall ask for permission every time that the program requests access

Firewalls are available as stand-alone programs (including a number of free versions for both Windows and Linux) or they are often bundled with anti-virus software. Additionally, Windows XP comes with a built-in firewall, but, as is the case with Windows

Internet Explorer, it will be targeted by people looking for exploits – flaws in other firewalls may never be found, but flaws in a Microsoft firewall will be found and they will be exploited.

Exercises:

Open up a command prompt on your computer and enter:

netstat -aon (for Windows) or

netstat -apn (for Linux)

Match the PID numbers with program names and try to determine which programs on your computer are accessing the network. (This is something that you can try at home, also.)

7.2 Packet Sniffer

Netstat will tell you what programs are connected to the network, but it won't show you what data these programs are sending. A packet sniffer, however, gives you the means to record and study the actual data that the programs are sending through the network.

7.2.1 Sniffing

A packet sniffer will record the network traffic on your computer, allowing you to look at the data. Tcpdump (and its Windows port, windump) may be considered the archetypical packet sniffers, but we're going to use Ethereal for our examples, because its graphical interface is simpler, and it allows you to more quickly record and view a basic capture file.

If you don't already have Ethereal, it can be downloaded from www.ethereal.com. Note to Windows users: To use Ethereal on a Windows based system, you must first download and install the WinPcap packet capture driver. WinPcap is available on the Ethereal download page or you can go to www.winpcap.polito.it to download it directly. Shut down all other applications, then start Ethereal. In the menu click on View then Autoscroll in Live Capture.

Next, click on Capture, then Start to go to the Capture Options screen. On the Capture Options screen, make sure that the box marked "Capture packets in promiscuous mode" is not checked, that the three check boxes under "Name Resolution" are checked, and that the box marked "Update list of packets in real time" is checked.

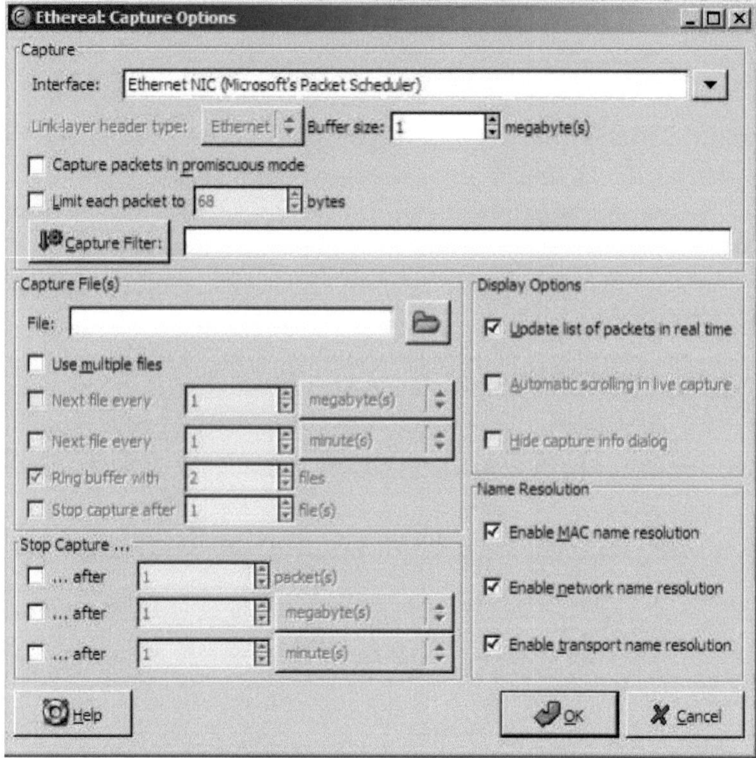

Now, click on the "OK" button.

In theory, nothing should happen now. You'll see a window for Ethereal which displays the number of packets that have been captured, and, behind this, you'll see the Ethereal screen which displays the data in those packets. You may see a small amount of traffic that is caused by the computers on the local network trying to keep track of each other (ARP, NBNS, ICMP) followed by DNS activity as Ethereal attempts to resolve names.

To see activity, you're going to generate some activity. While Ethereal is running, open your web browser. Minimize everything other than the main Ethereal screen and your web browser, and arrange the Ethereal and web browser windows so that you can see both at the same time. Now go to a web search engine, such as www.google.com.

As the web page loads, your should see information about captured packets scrolling up through the Ethereal screen. Pick a search term and enter it into the search bar. Click on some of the web pages that are brought up by the search and watch what happens in Ethereal as you do.

Note: If Ethereal reports no network activity at all, you may have the wrong network interface chosen. Go to the Interface drop-down list in the Capture Options screen and choose a different network interface.

7.2.2 Decoding Network Traffic

Now that you can see the network data that's moving through your computer, you have to figure out how to decode it.

In Ethereal, the first step, before you even end the capture session, is to look at the summary capture screen that the program displays while it is performing the capture. For our web browsing session, most of the packets should have been TCP packets (although if you stopped to watch a streaming video, your UDP packet numbers will have been increased). However, if you're capturing a simple web browsing session, and you see a large number of ARP or ICMP packets, that could indicate a problem.

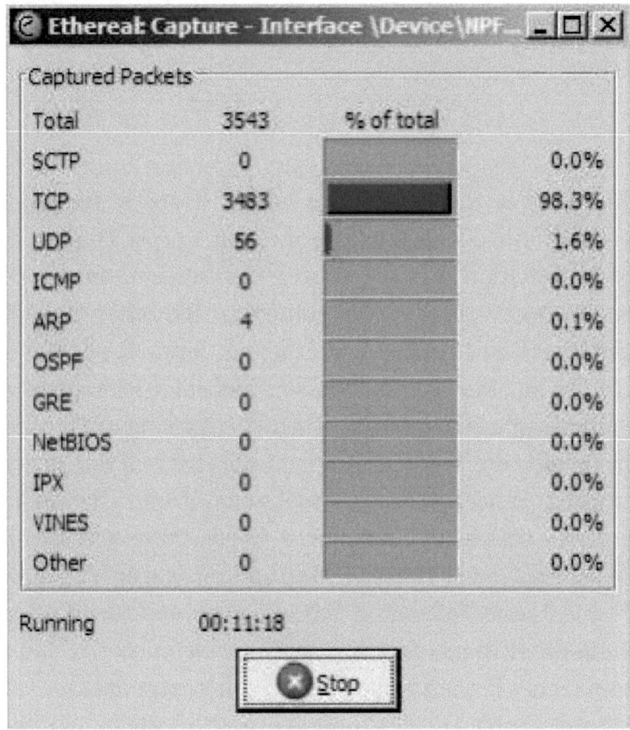

After you've ended the capture session, you're going to see output similar to this:

No.	Time	Source	Destination	Protocol	Info
1	0.000000	257.10.3.250	rodan.mozilla.org	TCP	1656 > 8080 [SYN] Seq=0 Ack=0 Win=16384 Len=0 MSS=1460
2	0.045195	257.10.3.250	rheet.mozilla.org	TCP	1657 > http [SYN] Seq=0 Ack=0 Win=16384 Len=0 MSS=1460
3	0.335194	rheet.mozilla.org	257.10.3.250	TCP	http > 1657 [SYN, ACK] Seq=0 Ack=1 Win=5840 Len=0 MSS=1460
4	0.335255	257.10.3.250	rheet.mozilla.org	TCP	1657 > http [ACK] Seq=1 Ack=1 Win=17520 Len=0
5	0.338234	257.10.3.250	rheet.mozilla.org	HTTP	GET /products/firefox/start/ HTTP/1.1
6	0.441049	rheet.mozilla.org	257.10.3.250	TCP	http > 1657 [ACK] Seq=1 Ack=580 Win=6948 Len=0
7	0.441816	rheet.mozilla.org	257.10.3.250	HTTP	HTTP/1.1 304 Not Modified
8	0.559132	257.10.3.250	rheet.mozilla.org	TCP	1657 > http [ACK] Seq=580 Ack=209 Win=17312 Len=0

9	2.855975	257.10.3.250	rodan.mozilla.org	TCP	1656 > 8080 [SYN] Seq=0 Ack=0 Win=16384 Len=0 MSS=1460
10	4.475529	257.10.3.250	name.server.com	DNS	Standard query PTR 250.3.10.257.in-addr.arpa
11	4.475776	257.10.3.250	name.server.com	DNS	Standard query PTR 205.111.126.207.in-addr.arpa
12	4.475854	257.10.3.250	name.server.com	DNS	Standard query PTR 202.111.126.207.in-addr.arpa

In this example, these twelve packets illustrate the web browser's activity as it connects with its specified start page. The most easily decoded information is in the Source and Destination columns. IP address 257.10.3.250 is the local computer; the other IP addresses have been resolved to names by Ethereal. Since the web browser used was the Mozilla Firefox browser, and since its start page was the default Mozilla Firefox page, it is not surprising to see addresses from the mozilla.org domain. The requests sent to name.server.com were probably generated by Ethereal when it sent DNS queries to resolve the IP addresses into names. (Note: these accesses by the Ethereal program were caused by the options you set in the Display Options and Name Resolution boxes. They were set to on in this example in order to produce a more readable output. If you toggle these options to off, then you won't have this extra data.)

Looking at source and destination information can help you spot unauthorized activity. For example, an unfamiliar domain name that is repeatedly accessed might indicate that you have a spyware program installed.

The next column is the Protocol column, which tells you what protocol the packets used. Again, to know when something is wrong here, you're going to have to know what to expect. In our web browsing session, we expect TCP and HTTP, and we understand why the DNS packets are there, but, for example, a large number of ICMP packets could mean that your machine is being pinged or traced.

The last column, Info, provides more detailed information about the packets. Packets 2, 3 and 4 show the TCP three-handed handshake of SYN, SYN/ACK, ACK, which indicates that a connection has been made. Packet 5 shows an HTTP GET command followed in packet 7 by a 304 Not Modified response.

If you want more information about the packets, the bottom two panes in the Ethereal screen show detailed explanations. The middle pane shows the details of the packet header. The bottom pane shows a hex and ascii dump of the data in the packet.

7.2.3 Sniffing Other Computers

Some of you, having looked at the information in this section – and having looked at the data that can be recorded by Ethereal, may be wondering about the possibilities of using packet sniffing software to record activity on other people's computers. Is this possible? Yes – and no. It's called promiscuous mode and it allows a packet sniffer to monitor network activity for all computers on a network.

This means that you might be able to record network activity on another computer that is in your own network (depending on the way that the hardware is set up), but you can't pick any one computer at random and magically sniff their data – the two computers must be physically connected, and the hardware and software must be properly configured.

7.2.4 Intrusion Detection Systems

You've probably realized that, to use a packet sniffer to detect unauthorized activity in real time, would require you to sit at your computer, watching the output of the packet sniffer and desperately hoping to see some kind of pattern. An intrusion detection system performs this task for you. These programs combine the ability to record network activity with sets of rules that allow them to flag unauthorized activity and generate real-time warnings.

Exercises:

1. Open Ethereal and start a live capture. Now open your web browser and look for a plain text document to download. Download and save the text file to your hard drive, then close the web browser

and end the capture session in Ethereal. Look through the packets captured by Ethereal, paying close attention to the ASCII dump in the bottom pane. What do you see?

If you have access to an email account, try checking your email while Ethereal is performing a capture. What do you see there?

2. Open Ethereal. On the Capture Options Screen, make sure that the box marked "Capture packets in promiscuous mode" is checked. This option may allow you to capture packets directed to or coming from other computers. Begin the capture and see what happens. Do you see any traffic that is intended for a computer other than yours?

What do you know about the hardware that connects your computer to the network? Does it connect to the other computers through a switch, a router or a hub? Go to a web search engine and try to find out which piece or pieces of hardware would make it most difficult to capture packets from other computers. What hardware would make it easiest?

3. Go to www.snort.org, or use a web search engine to research intrusion detection systems. How are they different from firewalls? What do they have in common with packet sniffers? What kinds of unauthorized activity can they detect? What kinds of activity might they be unable to detect?

7.3 Honeypots and Honeynets

People who like to watch monkeys go to the zoo, because there might be monkeys there. People who like to watch birds put out bird feeders, and the birds come to them. People who like to watch fish build aquariums, and bring the fish to themselves. But what do you do if you want to watch hackers?

You put out a honeypot.

Think about it this way – you're a bear. You may not know much (being a bear) but you do know that honey is tasty, and there is nothing better on a warm summer day than a big handful of honey. So you see a big pot full of honey sitting out in the center of a clearing, and you're thinking, 'Yum!" But once you stick your paw in the honey pot, you risk getting stuck. If nothing else, you're going to leave big, sticky paw prints everywhere, and everyone is going to know that someone has been in the honey, and there's a good chance that anyone who follows the big, sticky paw prints is going to discover that it's you. More than one bear has been trapped because of his affection for tasty honey.

A honeypot is a computer system, network, or virtual machine that serves no other purpose than to lure in hackers. In a honeypot, there are no authorized users – no real data is stored in the system, no real work is performed on it – so, every access, every attempt to use it, can be identified as unauthorized. Instead of sifting through logs to identify intrusions, the system administrator knows that every access is an intrusion, so a large part of the work is already done.

7.3.1 Types of Honeypots

There are two types of honeypots: production and research.

Production honeypots are used primarily as warning systems. A production honeypot identifies an intrusion and generates an alarm. They can show you that an intruder has identified the system or network as an object of interest, but not much else. For example, if you wanted to know if bears lived near your clearing, you might set out ten tiny pots of honey. If you checked them in the morning and found one or more of them empty, then you would know that bears had been in the vicinity, but you wouldn't know anything else about the bears.

Research honeypots are used to collect information about hacker's activities. A research honeypot lures in hackers, then keeps them occupied while it quietly records their actions. For example, if – instead of simply documenting their presence – you wanted to study the bears, then you might set out one big, tasty, sticky pot of honey in the middle of your clearing, but then you would surround that pot with movie cameras, still cameras, tape recorders and research assistants with clipboards and pith helmets.

The two types of honeypots differ primarily in their complexity. You can more easily set up and maintain a production honeypot because of its simplicity and the limited amount of information that you hope to collect. In a production honeypot, you just want to know that you've been hit; you don't care so much whether the hackers stay around, However, in a research honeypot, you want the hackers to stay, so that you can see what they are doing. This makes setting up and maintaining a research honeypot more difficult, because you must make the system look like a real, working system that offers files or services that the hackers find interesting. A bear who knows what a honeypot looks like, might spend a minute looking at an empty pot, but only a full pot full of tasty honey is going to keep the bear hanging around long enough for you to study it.

7.3.2 Building a Honeypotd

In the most basic sense, a honeypot is nothing more than a computer system which is set up with the expectation that it will be compromised by intruders. Essentially, this means that if you connect a computer with a insecure operating system to the Internet, then let it sit there, waiting to be compromised, you have created a honeypot! But this isn't a very useful honeypot.

It's more like leaving your honey out in the clearing, then going home to the city. When you come back, the honey will be gone, but you won't know anything about who, how, when or why. You don't learn anything from your honeypot, useless you have some way of gathering information regarding it. To be useful, even the most basic honeypot most have some type of intrusion detection system. The intrusion detection system could be as simple as a firewall. Normally a firewall is used to prevent unauthorized users from accessing a computer system, but they also log everything that passes through or is stopped. Reviewing the logs produced by the firewall can provide basic information about attempts to access the honeypot. More complex honeypots might add hardware, such as switches, routers or hubs, to further monitor or control network access.

They may also use packet sniffers to gather additional information about network traffic. Research honeypots may also run programs that simulate normal use, making it appear that the honeypot is actually being accessed by authorized users, and teasing potential intruders with falsified emails, passwords and data. These types of programs can also be used to disguise operating systems, making it appear, for example, that a Linux based computer is running Windows.

But the thing about honey – it's sticky, and there's always a chance that your honeypot is going to turn into a bees nest. And when the bees come home, you don't want to be the one with your hand stuck in the honey. An improperly configured honeypot can easily be turned into a launching pad for additional attacks. If a hacker compromises your honeypot, then promptly launches an assault on a large corporation or uses your honeypot to distribute a flood of spam, there's a good chance that you will be identified as the one responsible.

Correctly configured honeypots control network traffic going into and out of the computer. A simple production honeypot might allow incoming traffic through the firewall, but stop all outgoing traffic. This is a simple, effective solution, but intruders will quickly realize that is is not a real, working computer system. A slightly more complex honeypot might allow some outgoing traffic, but not all. Research honeypots – which want to keep the intruders interested as long as possible – sometimes use manglers, which audit outgoing traffic and disarm potentially dangerous data by modifying it so that it is ineffective.

Exercises:

Honeypots can be useful tools for research and for spotting intruders, but using them to capture and prosecute these intruders is another question. Different jurisdictions have different definitions and standards, and judges and juries often have varying views, so there are many questions that need to be considered. Do honeypots represent an attempt at entrapment? Is recording a hacker's activities a form of wiretapping?

And on the specific question of honeypots – can it be illegal to compromise a system that was designed to be compromised? These questions have yet to be thoroughly tested.

Discuss your opinions on the legalities of using honeypots for capturing hackers involved in criminal activities. Do you think it would be a useful tool for law enforcement agencies? Is it entrapment? Do you think it constitutes an 'attractive nuisance'? If a hacker comprises a honeypot, who do you think is ultimately responsible?

VIII

DIGITAL FORENSICS

8.0 Introduction

Forensics concerns the application of a methodical investigation technique in order to reconstruct a sequence of events. Most people are now familiar with the concept of forensics from TV and films, “CSI (Crime Scene Investigation)” being one of the most popular. Forensic science was for a long time – and still is really – most associated with Forensic Pathology – finding out how people died. The first recorded description of forensics was on just this subject In 1248, a Chinese book called Hsi DuanYu (the Washing Away of Wrongs) was published. This book describes how to tell if someone has drowned or has been strangled.

Digital forensics is a bit less messy and a bit less well known. This is the art of recreating what has happened in a digital device. In the past it was restricted to computers only, but now encompasses all digital devices such as mobile phones, digital cameras, and even GPS 2 devices. It has been used to catch murderers, kidnappers, fraudsters, Mafia bosses and many other decidedly unfriendly people.

In this lesson, we are going to cover two aspects of forensics (all computer based I‘m afraid – no mobile phone stuff here).

1. What people have been up to on their own computer. This covers ...

- the recovery of deleted files.
- elementary decryption.
- searching for certain file types.
- searching for certain phrases.
- looking at interesting areas of the computer.

2. What a remote user has been doing on someone else's computer.

This covers

- reading log files.
- reconstructing actions.
- tracing the source.

This lesson is going to focus on the tools available under Linux. There are tools that are available under Windows, as well as dedicated software and hardware for doing forensics, but with the capability of Linux to mount and understand a large number of alternate operating and file systems, it is the ideal environment for most forensic operations.

1 Apparently it is something to do with marks left around the throat, and the level of water penetration into the lungs.

2 Global Positioning System – a thing which tell you where you are in the world using a number of orbiting satellites.

8.1 Forensic Principles

8.1.0 Introduction

There are a number of basic principles that are necessary regardless of whether you are examining a computer or a corpse. This section is a quick summary of these principals.

8.1.1 Avoid Contamination

On TV you see forensic examiners dressed up in white suits with gloves, handling all evidence with tweezers and putting it into sealed plastic bags. This is all to prevent "contamination". This is where evidence is tainted, for example, by fingerprints being added to the handle of a knife by someone picking it up (think The Fugitive if you have seen it ... Look what trouble it got him into !)

8.1.2 Act Methodically

Whatever you do, when (if ?) you get to court, you will need to justify all the actions that you have taken. If you act in a scientific and methodical manner, making careful notes of what it is that you are doing and how you do it, this justification becomes much easier. It also allows for someone else to follow your steps and verify that you haven't made a mistake which may cast the value of your evidence in doubt.

8.1.3 Chain of Evidence

You must maintain something called the "Chain of Evidence". This means that at any point in time from the seizure of the evidence until it's final presentation in court, that you can account for who has had access to it, and where it has been. This rules out the possibility that someone has tampered with it, or falsified it in some way,

8.1.4 Conclusion

Keep these things in mind, and even if you are not going to take your work to court, you will be able to maximize your abilities as a forensic examiner.

8.2 Stand-alone Forensics

8.2.0 Introduction

This section is about the forensic examination of an individual machine. For want of a better term, we will call it "stand-alone forensics". This is probably the most common part of computer forensics - its main role is to find out what has been done using a particular computer. The forensic examiner could be looking for evidence of fraud, such as financial spreadsheets, evidence of communication with someone else, e-mails or an address book, or evidence of a particular nature, such as pornographic images.

8.2.1 Hard Drive and Storage Media Basics

There are several components that make up an average computer. There is the processor, memory, graphics cards, CD drives and much more. One of the most crucial components is the harddisk (hard drive). This is where a majority of the information that the computer requires to operate is stored.

The Operating System (OS) such as Windows or Linux resides here, along with user applications such as word processors and games. This is also where significant amounts of data is stored, either deliberately, through the action of saving a file, or incidentally, through the use of temporary files and caches. This allows a forensic examiner to reconstruct the actions that a computer user has carried out on a computer, which files have been accessed and much, much more.

There are several levels at which you can examine a harddisk. For the purposes of this exercise, we are only going to look at the file system level. It is worth noting though, that professionals are capable of looking in a great level of detail at a disk to determine what it used to contain – even if it has been overwritten many times.

The file system is the computer's implementation of a filing cabinet. It contains drawers (partitions), files (directories) and individual pieces of paper (files).

Files and directories can be hidden, although this is only a superficial thing and can easily be overcome. Working through the following Exercises should give you a far better understanding of the basics of disk storage.

Exercises:

For each of the following terms about storage media, search for information and learn how they work. Understanding how equipment functions normally is your first step toward forensics.

1. Magnetic/Hard/Physical Disk: This is where your computer stores files. Explain how magnetism is used on a hard disk.
2. Tracks: What are referred to as "tracks on a hard disk?
3. Sectors: This is a fixed space that data fits into. Explain how.
4. Cluster/Allocation unit: Explain why when a file is written to a hard disk that it may be assigned more space than it needs. What happens to that empty space? Looking up the term "file slack" should help you.
5. Free/"Unallocated" Space: This is what you have left after files are deleted. Or are those files really gone? Explain how a file is deleted on the computer. Looking for tools on "secure delete" may help you. Knowing how you are supposed to securely delete a file so it's really gone is a great way to learn why such tools are needed.
6. Hash, also known as an MD5 hash: Explain what this hash is and what it's used for.
7. BIOS: This stands for "Basic Input/Output System". What is this and where is it stored on a PC?
8. Boot Sector: This works with partition tables to help your PC find the operating system to run. There are many tools for working with partitions, with the standard one being called fdisk. Knowing how these tools work is your first clue to understanding partitions and the boot sector.

9. Cyclical Redundancy Check (CRC): When you get a "read error" message from your hard disk, this means that the data failed a CRC check. Find out what the CRC check is and what it does.

10. File Signature: Often times a file has a small 6-byte signature at the start of the file which identifies what kind of file it is. Opening a file in a text-editor is the easiest way to see this. Open 3 files of each of the following file types in a text editor: .jpg, .gif, .exe, .mp3. What was the first word at the top of the file for each?

11. RAM (Random-Access Memory): This is also known as "memory" and it is a temporary location to read and write information. It is much, much faster than writing to the hard disk. It's also gone when power is lost to the computer. Explain how RAM works. Knowing your computer may have anywhere from 64 to 512 Mb of RAM, search for information about a computer that has more RAM than that.

12. Currently, the largest RAM disk (a super fast hard disk emulated in RAM) is 2.5 Tb (Terabyte). How many times larger than your PC is that?

8.2.2 Encryption, Decryption and File Formats

A lot of the files that you will come across will not be immediately readable. Many programs have their own proprietary file formats, while others use standard formats – for example the standard picture formats - gif, jpeg, etc. Linux provides an excellent utility to help you to determine what a given file is. It is called file.

Command Line Switch	Effect
-k	Don't stop at the first match, keep going.
-L	Follow symbolic links
-z	Attempt to look inside compressed files.

An example of the use of the file command is shown below:

```
[simon@frodo file_example]$ ls
arp.c                   nwrap.pl
isestorm_DivX.avi       oprp_may11_2004.txt
krb5-1.3.3              VisioEval.exe
krb5-1.3.3.tar          Windows2003.vmx
krb5-1.3.3.tar.gz.asc
[simon@frodo file_example]$ file *
arp.c:                         ASCII C program text
```

```
isestorm_DivX.avi:             RIFF (little-endian) data, AVI
krb5-1.3.3:                    directory
krb5-1.3.3.tar:                POSIX tar archive
krb5-1.3.3.tar.gz.asc:         PGP armored data
nwrap.pl:                      Paul Falstad's zsh script text
executable
oprp_may11_2004.txt:           ASCII English text, with very long
lines, with CRLF line terminators
VisioEval.exe:                 MS-DOS executable (EXE), OS/2 or MS
Windows
Windows2003.vmx:               a /usr/bin/vmware script text
executable
[simon@frodo file_example]$
```

From this you can start to make some attempts to read a certain type of file. There are a number of file conversion utilities available to you under Linux, and even more available on the Internet, as well as a number of file viewers for various formats. Sometimes it may require more than one step to get to a place where you can really work with the data – try to think laterally!

Occasionally, you will come across files which have been encrypted or password protected. The complication that this presents varies, from encryption that is easily broken to stuff that would even give the NSA (or GCHQ or whatever your local government agency happens to be) a headache. There are again a number of tools available on the Internet that you can use to try to break the encryption on a file. It pays to examine the area surrounding the computer that you are dealing with. People aren't very good at remembering passwords, it may well be written down somewhere nearby. Common choices for passwords also involve : pets, relatives, dates (marriage, date of birth), telephone numbers, car registrations, and other simple combinations (123456, abcdef, qwerty etc.). People are also reluctant to use more than one or two passwords for everything, so if you can reverse engineer a password on one file or application, try it on the others. It is highly likely to be the same.

Exercises:

For these Exercises, we will learn about password cracking. While it is legal to crack your own passwords if you forget them, it is not legal in some countries to figure out how something else is encrypted, in order to protect the other material from being cracked.

DVD movies are encrypted to prevent them from being stolen off the DVD and sold. While this is an excellent use of encryption, it is illegal for anyone to research how that encryption is used. This leads to your first exercise:

1. What is "DeCSS" and how does it relate to DVD encryption? Search on "decss" to learn more.

2. Knowing that something is password protected means learning how to open that file. This is known as "cracking" the password. Find information about cracking various types of passwords. To do this search for "cracking XYZ passwords" where XYZ is the password type you are looking for. Do this for the

following password types:

- MD5
- Adobe PDF
- Excel

3. If the encryption method is too strong to be broken, it may be necessary to perform a "dictionary attack" (sometimes known as "brute force"). Find out what a dictionary attack is.

8.2.3 Finding a Needle in a Haystack

Commercial forensic software includes powerful search tools that allow you to search for many combinations and permutations of factors. Without these expensive commercial tools you need to be a little more resourceful. Linux provides you with plenty of scope to construct similar tools using standard utilities. The following text details the use of find, grep and strings, and then describes the use of the pipe to combine them.

8.2.3.1 find

find [path...][expression]

find is used to locate files meeting certain criteria within the operating system. It is not designed for looking within the files. There must be a million permutations of expressions that can be combined to search for a file.

Exercise:

1. Read the manual page for find. Complete the "Effect" for each "Expression" in the table below. (Hint: Where a number is given as an argument, it can be specified as follows: +n – for greater than n; -n – for less than n; n – for exactly n.)

Expression	Effect
-amin n	File last accessed n minutes ago
-anewer	
-atime	
-cnewer	
-iname	
-inum	
-name	
-regex	
-size	
-type	
-user	

8.2.3.2 grep

grep is an immensely powerful tool. It is used to find certain lines within a file. This allows you to quickly find files that contain certain things within a directory or file system. It also allows for searching on regular expressions. There are search patterns that allow you to specify criteria that the search must match. For example: finding all strings in the dictionary that start with "s" and finish with "t" to help with doing a crossword.

grep ^s.*t$ /usr/share/dict/words

Exercises:

1. Read the manual page for grep.
2. Look up regular expressions for grep on the Internet. Try to construct a regular expression that looks for all words that are four letters long and contain an "a".

8.2.3.3 strings

strings is another useful utility. This will search through a file of any type for human readable strings. This can return a great deal of information about a specific file, often providing information about the application that created it, authors, original creation time and so on.

Exercise:

1. Read the manual page for strings.

8.2.3.4 awk

awk is a programming language designed for working with strings. It is used to extract information from one command to feed into another. For example, to take just the running programs from the ps command, you would use the following:

```
ps | awk '{print $4}'
```

Exercise:

1. Read the manual page for awk.

8.2.3.5 The Pipe "|"

All of the above tools are easily combined using the UNIX "pipe" command. This is shown with the "|" symbol. This allows you to take the output of one command and feed it down a pipe to another command. To find all files in the current directory that are mpg files, use the following:

```
ls | grep mpg
```

Exercises:

1. Using the pipe, the ls command and grep, find all files in the current directory that were created this month.

2. Using the ps command and awk, print a list of all the running process names.

8.2.4 Making use of other sources

There are many other interesting ways of examining how a computer has been used. Nearly every application that gets run will record some additional data beyond the files that it directly takes in, or files that it puts out. This could include temporary files for processing, lists of last accessed files or the history of a web-browser.

Exercises:

1. What is browser cache? Find the location where your web browser stores its cache.

2. What are browser cookies? Find the location where your web browser stores its cookies.

3. Search for information about web browser cookies. What kinds of cookies are there and what kind of information is stored in them?

4. Your computer uses temporary directories where it writes files by default for the user. This is often times known as Application Data. Find the temporary directories you have available on your computer. While may be called tmp or temp, often times, there are many more that you don't know about. Try FIND on files written with today's date as a great way to find temporary files. Do those files disappear when you reboot the computer?

8.3 Network Forensics

8.3.0 Introduction

Network forensics is used to find out where a computer is located and to prove whether a particular file was sent from a particular computer. While network forensics can be very complicated, we will cover some of the basics that can be applied to everyday life.

8.3.1 Firewall Logs

Who's connecting to me? The firewall is a utility which can choke connections between two points in a network. Many types of firewalls exist. Regardless of the type and job of the firewall, it is the firewall logs which give you the details. Only by using the logs, can you find patterns of attacks and abuse to your firewall.

Exercises:

1. Visit the website http://www.dshield.org. This website takes firewall logs from all over the world to find patterns of network attack attempts. This helps security professionals be sure to verify if the networks they are protecting are vulnerable to those particular attacks before they happen. Read through the website and explain how that pie graph of the world is made and what it means.
2. On the same website, read through the "Fight back" section and the response e-mails they receive. Explain the purpose of this.

8.3.2 Mail Headers

E-mails come with information of every computer they pass through to get to you. This is kept in the headers. Sometimes even more information is in the headers. To view the headers however is not always so simple. Various mail clients will all have different ways to view this. The real trick to reading headers, though, is to know they are backwards. The top of the list is you. Then it travels goes with each line until the very last line is the computer or network that the mail was sent from.

Exercises:

1. A great resource focused on network forensics for fighting SPAM is http://www.samspade.org. Visit SamSpade.org and go to the section called "The Library". Using this section you should be able to explain how to read e-mail headers. You should also read about forged e-mail headers and e-mail abuse. Explain the various ways e-mail can be used to cause harm.

2. Determine how to look at your e-mail headers in the e-mails you receive. Are there any particular fields in those headers that seem foreign to you? Look them up. You should be able to explain what each field means in that header.

IX
E-MAIL SECURITY

9.0 Introduction

Everyone uses e-mail. It is the second most used application on the internet next to your web browser. But what you might not realize is that a significant portion of network attacks and compromises originate through e-mail. And with respect to your privacy, misuse of e-mail has the potential to disclose either the contents of your message, or give a spammer information about you. The purpose of this module is to give you information on how e-mail works, safe e-mail usage, e-mail based attacks, and security strategies for e-mail.

9.1 How E-mail Works

Just like airmail is sent through the air, 'e'-mail is sent through the 'e' – the 'e' in this case being the web of electronic connections within and between the networks that make up the Internet. When you send an e-mail from your computer, the data is sent from your computer to an SMTP server. The SMTP server then searches for the correct POP3 server and sends your e-mail to that server, where it waits until your intended recipient retrieves it.

9.1.1 E-mail Accounts

E-mail accounts are available through many different sources. You may get one through school, through your work or through your ISP. When you get an e-mail account, you will be given a two part e-mail address, in this form: username@domain.name. The first part, username identifies you on your network, differentiating you from all the other users on the network. The second part, domain.name is used to identify your specific network. The username must be unique within your network, just as the domain name must be unique among all the other networks on the Internet.

However, user names are not unique outside of their networks; it is possible for two users on two different networks to share user names. For example, if there is one user with the address bill@bignetwork.net, there will not be another user on bignetwork.net whose user name is bill. However, bill@bignetwork.net and bill@smallnetwork.net are both valid e-mail addresses that can refer to different users. One of the first things that you will do when you are setting up your e-mail is to enter your e-mail address into your e-mail client program. Your e-mail client is the program that you will use to send and receive e-mails. Microsoft's Outlook Express may be the most widely known (since it comes free with every copy of a Microsoft operating system), but there are many others available for both Windows and Linux, including Mozilla, Eudora, Thunderbird and Pine.

9.1.2 POP and SMTP

After your e-mail client knows your e-mail address, it's going to need to know where to look for incoming e-mail and where to send outgoing e-mail. Your incoming e-mails are going to be on a computer called a POP server.

The POP server – usually named something like pop.smallnetwork.net or mail.smallnetwork.net – has a file on it that is associated with your e-mail address and which contains e-mails that have been sent to you from someone else. POP stands for post office protocol. Your outgoing e-mails will be sent to a computer called a SMTP server.

This server – named smtp.smallnetwork.net – will look at the domain name contained in the e-mail address of any e-mails that you send, then will perform a DNS lookup to determine which POP3 server it should send the e-mail to. SMTP stands for simple mail transfer protocol.

When you start up your e-mail client, a number of things happen:

1. When you start up your e-mail client, a number of things happen:
2. the client sends your secret password to the POP server
3. the client sends your secret password to the POP server
4. the client sends your outgoing e-mail to the SMTP server.

The first thing to note is that you do not send a password to the SMTP server. SMTP is an old protocol, designed in the early days of e-mail, at a time when almost everyone on the Internet knew each other personally. The protocol was written with the assumption that everyone who would be using it would be trustworthy, so SMTP doesn't check to ensure that you are you. Most SMTP servers use other methods to authenticate users, but – in theory – anyone can use any SMTP server to send e-mail. (For more information on this, see section.

9.2.4 Forged Headers.)

The second thing to note is that, when you send your secret password to the POP server, you send it in a plain-text format. It may be hidden by little asterisks on your computer screen, but it is transmitted through the network in an easily readable format. Anyone who is monitoring traffic on the network – using a packet sniffer, for instance – will be able to clearly see your password.

You may feel certain that your network is safe, but you have little control over what might be happening on any other network through which your data may pass. The third, and possibly most important thing that you need to know about your e-mails, is that they are – just like your password – transmitted and stored in a plain-text format. It is possible that they may be monitored any time they are transferred from the server to your computer.

This all adds up to one truth: e-mail is not a secure method of transferring information. Sure, it's great for relaying jokes, and sending out spunkball warnings, but, if you're not comfortable yelling something out through the window to your neighbor, then maybe you should think twice about putting it in an e-mail. Does that sound paranoid? Well, yeah, it is paranoid, but that doesn't necessarily make it untrue.

Much of our e-mail communications are about insignificant details. No one but you, Bob and Alice, care about your dinner plans for next Tuesday. And, even if Carol desperately wants to know where you and Bob and Alice are eating next Tuesday, the odds are slim that she has a packet sniffer running on any of the networks your e-mail might pass through. But, if a company is known to use e-mail to arrange for credit card transactions, it is not unlikely to assume that someone has, or is trying to, set up a method to sniff those credit card numbers out of the network traffic.

9.1.3 Web Mail

A second option for e-mail is to use a web based e-mail account. This will allow you to use a web browser to check your e-mail. Since the e-mail for these accounts is normally stored on the web e-mail server – not on your local computer – it is very convenient to use these services from multiple computers.

It is possible that your ISP will allow you to access your e-mail through both POP and the web. However, you must remember that web pages are cached or stored on local computers, sometimes for significant lengths of time. If you check your e-mail through a web based system on someone else's computer, there is a good chance that your e-mails will be accessible to someone else who uses that computer.

Web based e-mail accounts are often free and easy to get. This means that they offer an opportunity for you to have several identities online. You can, for instance, have one e-mail address that you use only for friends and another that is only for relatives. This is usually considered acceptable, as long as you are not intentionally intending to defraud anyone.

Exercises:

1. You can learn a lot about how POP e-mail is retrieved by using the telnet program. When you use telnet instead of an e-mail client, you have to enter all the commands by hand (commands that the e-mail client program usually issues automatically). Using a web search engine, find the instructions and commands necessary to access an e-mail account using the telnet program. What are the drawbacks to using this method to retrieve e-mail? What are some of the potential advantages?

2. Find three organizations that offer web based e-mail services. What, if any, promises do they make about the security of e-mail sent or received using their services? Do they make any attempts to authenticate their users?

3. (possibly homework) Determine the SMTP server for the email address you use most frequently.

9.2 Safe E-mail Usage Part 1: Receiving

Everyone uses e-mail, and to the surprise of many people, your e-mail can be used against you. E-mail should be treated as a post card, in that anyone who looks can read the contents. You should never put anything in an ordinary e-mail that you don't want to be read. That being said there are strategies for securing your e-mail. In this section we will cover safe and sane e-mail usage and how to protect your privacy online.

9.2.1 Spam, Phishing and Fraud

Everybody likes to get e-mail. A long time ago, in a galaxy far far away it used to be you only got mail from people you knew, and it was about things you cared about. Now you get e-mail from people you never heard of asking you to buy software, drugs, and real estate, not to mention help them get 24 million dollars out of Nigeria. This type of unsolicited advertising is called spam. It comes as a surprise to many people that e-mail they receive can provide a lot of information to a sender, such as when the mail was opened and how many times it was read, if it was forwarded, etc.

This type of technology – called web bugs – is used by both spammers and legitimate senders. Also, replying to an e-mail or clicking on the unsubscribe link may tell the sender that they have reached a live address. Another invasion of privacy concern is the increasingly common "phishing" attack. Have you ever gotten an e-mail asking you to login and verify your bank or E-bay account information? Beware, because it is a trick to steal your account information. To secure yourself against these types of attacks, there are some simple strategies to protect yourself outlined below.

9.2.2 HTML E-Mail

One of the security concerns with HTML based e-mail is the use of web bugs. Web bugs are hidden images in your e-mail that link to the senders' web server, and can provide them with notification that you have received or opened the mail. Another flaw with HTML e-mail is that the sender can embed links in the e-mail that identify the person who clicks on them. This can give the sender information about the status of the message. As a rule, you should use a mail client that allows you to disable the automatic downloading of attached or embedded images.

Another problem is related to scripts in the e-mail that may launch an application ,if your browser has not been patched for security flaws. For web based e-mail clients, you may have the option of disabling the automatic download of images, or viewing the message as text. Either is a good security practice. The best way to protect yourself against HTML e-mail based security and privacy attacks is to use text based e-mail. If you must use HTML e-mail, beware!

9.2.3 Attachment Security

Another real concern related to received e-mail security is attachments. Attackers can send you malware, viruses, Trojan horses and all sorts of nasty programs. The best defense against e-mail borne malware is to not open anything from anyone you don't know. Never open a file with the extension .exe or .scr, as these are extensions that will launch an executable file that may infect your computer with a virus. For good measure, any files you receive should be saved to your hard drive and scanned with an antivirus program. Beware of files that look like a well known file type, such as a zip file. Sometimes attackers can disguise a file by changing the icon or hiding the file extension so you don't know it is an executable.

9.2.4 Forged headers

Occasionally you may receive an e-mail that looks like it is from someone you know, or from the "Administrator" or "Postmaster" or "Security Team" at your school or ISP. The subject may be "Returned Mail" or "Hacking Activity" or some other interesting subject line. Often there will be an attachment. The problem is that it takes no technical knowledge and about 10 seconds of work to forge an e-mail address. (It also – depending on where you live – may be very illegal.)

To do this, you make a simple change to the settings in your e-mail client software. Where it asks you to enter your e-mail address (under Options, Settings or Preferences) you enter something else. From here on out, all your messages will have a fake return address. Does this mean that you're safe from identification? No, not really. Anyone with the ability to read an e-mail header and procure a search warrant can probably figure out your identity from the information contained on the header. What it does mean is that a spammer can represent himself as anyone he wants to. So if Fannie Gyotoku [telecommunicatecreatures@cox.net] sells you a magic cell phone antenna that turns out to be a cereal box covered with tin foil, you can complain to cox.net, but don't be surprised when they tell you that there is no such user.

Most ISPs authenticate senders and prevent relaying, which means that you have to be who you say you are to send mail via their SMTP server. The problem is that hackers and spammers often run an SMTP server on their PC, and thus don't have to authenticate to send e-mail, and can make it appear any way they want. The one sure way to know if a suspicious e-mail is legitimate is to know the sender and call them up. Never reply to a message that you suspect may be forged, as this lets the sender know they have reached an actual address. You can also look at the header information to determine where the mail came from, as in the following example:

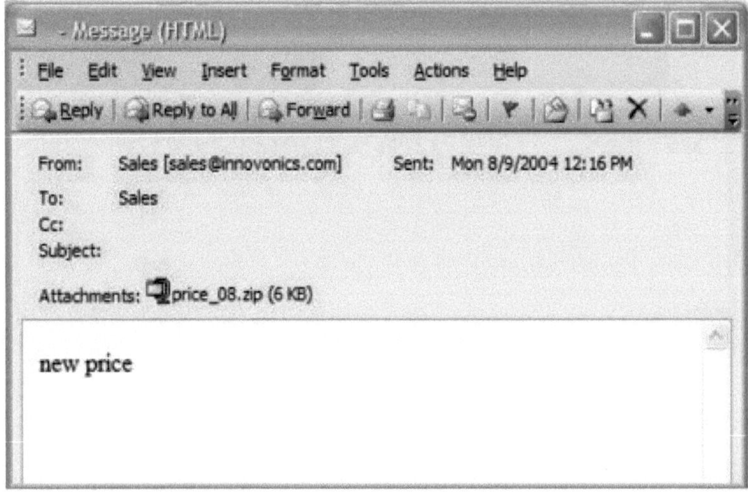

This is an e-mail from someone I don't know, with a suspicious attachment. Normally, I would just delete this but I want to know where it came from. So I'll look at the message header. I use Outlook 2003 as my e-mail client, and to view the header you go to view>options and you will see the header information as below:

Microsoft Mail Internet Headers Version 2.0

```
Received: from srv1.mycompany.com ([192.168.10.53]) by mx1.mycompany.com
over TLS secured channel with Microsoft SMTPSVC(6.0.3790.0);
        Mon, 9 Aug 2004 11:20:18 -0700
Received: from [10.10.205.241] (helo=www.mycompany.com)
      by srv1.mycompany.com with esmtp (Exim 4.30)
      id 1BuEgL-0001OU-8a; Mon, 09 Aug 2004 11:15:37 -0700
Received: from kara.org (67.108.219.194.ptr.us.xo.net [67.108.219.194])
      by www.mycompany.com (8.12.10/8.12.10) with SMTP id i79IBYUr030082
      for <sales@mycompany.com>; Mon, 9 Aug 2004 11:11:34 -0700
Date: Mon, 09 Aug 2004 14:15:35 -0500
To: "Sales" <sales@mycompany.com>
From: "Sales" <sales@innovonics.com>
Subject:
Message-ID: <cdkdabgurdgefupfhnt@mycompany.com>
MIME-Version: 1.0
Content-Type: multipart/mixed;
        boundary="--------cfwriebwwbnnfkkmojga"
X-Scan-Signature: 178bfa9974a422508674b1924a9c2835
Return-Path: sales@innovonics.com
X-OriginalArrivalTime: 09 Aug 2004 18:20:18.0890 (UTC) FILETIME=
[868FEAA0:01C47E3D]
----------cfwriebwwbnnfkkmojga
Content-Type: text/html; charset="us-ascii"
Content-Transfer-Encoding: 7bit
----------cfwriebwwbnnfkkmojga
Content-Type: application/octet-stream; name="price_08.zip"
Content-Transfer-Encoding: base64
Content-Disposition: attachment; filename="price_08.zip"
----------cfwriebwwbnnfkkmojga—
```

Now, the part I'm interested in is highlighted above. Note that the "Received" is from kara.org at an IP that appears to be an xo.net DSL line, which does not agree with innovonics.com, the purported sender.

Also, if I look up innovonics.com's mail server using nslookup, its address comes back as follows:

```
C:\>nslookup innovonics.com
Server:  dc.mycompany.com
Address:  192.168.10.54
```

Non-authoritative answer:
Name: innovonics.com
Address: 64.143.90.9

So, my suspicion was correct, and this is an e-mail that is carrying some malware in an executable file posing as a zip file. The malware has infected the person's computer on the DSL line, which is now a zombie, sending copies of the malware to everyone in the infected computers address book. I'm glad I checked it out!

Exercises:

1. Citbank and PayPal are two of the most common targets of phishing emails. Research what Citibank or PayPal are doing to fight / control phishing.

2. Research whether your bank or credit card holder has a published statement about the use of email and personal information.

3. (possibly homework) Research a spam email you have received and see if you can determine the real source.

9.3 Safe E-mail Usage Part 2: Sending

Sending mail is a little more care free. There are some things you can do to make sure your conversation is secure though. The first is to ensure your connection is secure (see section 9.4 Connection Security for more information). There are also methods to allow you to digitally sign your messages, which guarantees that the message is from you and has not been tampered with en route. And for maximum security, you can encrypt your messages to make sure no one reads them.

Digital signatures prove who e-mail comes from, and that it has not been altered in transit. If you establish the habit of using digital signatures for important e-mail, you will have a lot of credibility if you ever need to disown forged mail that appears to be from you. They also allow you to encrypt e-mail so that no one can read it except the recipient. PGP in particular offers high levels of encryption which to break would require extreme computing power.

9.3.1 Digital Certificates

A digital certificate is unique to an individual, kind of like a drivers license or passport, and is composed of 2 parts. These parts are a public and private key. The certificate is unique to one person, and typically certificates are issued by a trusted Certificate Authority, or CA. The list of Certificate Authorities you trust is distributed automatically (if you are a Microsoft Windows User) by Windows Update and the list is accessible in your browser under tools>internet options>content>certificates. You can go here to view certificates installed on your machine (yours and others), and other certificate authorities you trust.

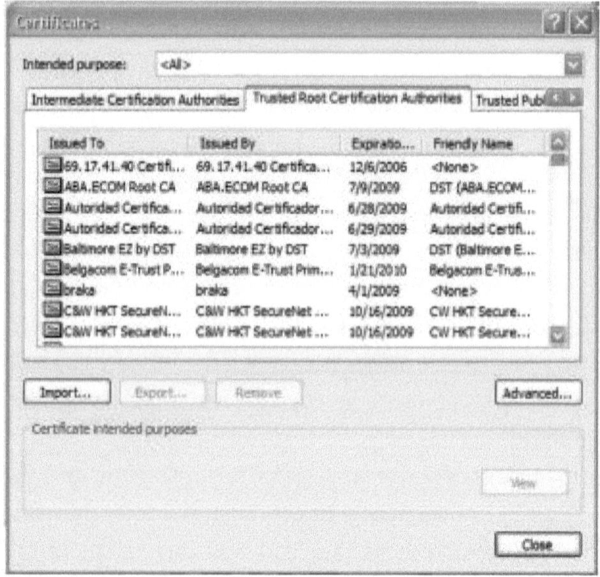

You can disable the automatic update of CAs, and choose to remove all CAs from the list, although this is not recommended. Instructions on how to do this are on Microsoft's web site.

9.3.2 Digital Signatures

A digital signature is generated by your e-mail software and your private key to assure the authenticity of your e-mail. The purpose of the signature is twofold. The first is to certify it came from you. This is called non-repudiation. The second is to ensure the contents have not been altered. This is called data integrity. The way an e-mail program accomplishes this is by running the contents of your message through a one way hash function. This produces a fixed size output of your e-mail called a message digest. This is a unique value, and if the mathematical algorithm that produces it is strong, the message digest has the following attributes.

- The original message can't be reproduced from the digest.
- Each digest is unique.

After the digest is created, it is encrypted with your private key. The encrypted digest is attached to the original message along with your public key. The recipient then opens the message, and the digest is decrypted with your public key. The digest is compared to an identical digest generated by the recipients' mail program. If they match, then you're done. If not, your mail client will let you know the message has been altered. There are 2 types of signing / encryption functions, S/MIME and PGP. S/MIME is considered to be the corporate and government choice, possibly because it uses the less labor intensive certificate authority model for authentication, and because it is more easily implemented through Microsoft's Outlook Express e-mail program. PGP is more often the choice of the computer user community, because it is based on a non-centralized web of trust for authentication, where a user's trustworthiness is validated through the 'friend of a friend' system, where you agree that, if you trust me, then you can also trust those people who I trust, and because members of the computer user community don't really care if it takes them four hours to figure out how to make PGP work with Thunderbird – they consider these types of challenges to be a form of recreation.

9.3.3 Getting a certificate

If you are interested in getting a digital certificate or digital ID, you need to contact a Certificate Authority (Verisign and thawte are the most well known, although a web search may find others.) Both require you to provide identification to prove to them that you are who you are. You can get a free certificate from thawte, but they require a significant amount of personal information, including a government identification number (such as a passport, tax id or driver's license). Verisign charges a fee for its certificate and requires that you pay this fee with a credit card, but asks for less personal information. (Presumably, Verisign is relying on the credit card company to validate your personal information.) These requests for information may seem intrusive, but remember, you are asking these companies to vouch for your trustworthiness. And – as always – check with your parents or guardians before you give out any personal information (or run up large balances on their credit cards).

The biggest disadvantage to using a certificate authority is that your private key is available to someone else – the certificate authority. If the certificate authority is compromised, then your digital ID is also compromised.

9.3.4 Encryption

As an additional layer of security, you can encrypt your e-mail. Encryption will turn your e-mail text into a garbled mess of numbers and letters that can only be read by its intended recipient. Your deepest secrets and your worst poetry will be hidden from all but the most trusted eyes.

However, you must remember, that, while this may sound good to you – and to all of us who don't really wish to be exposed to bad poetry – some governments do not approve. Their arguments may –

or may not – be valid (you can discuss this amongst yourselves), but validity is not the point. The point is that, depending on the laws of the nation in which you live, sending an encrypted e-mail may be a crime, regardless of the content.

9.3.5 How does it work?

Encryption is fairly complicated, so I'll try to explain it in a low tech way:

Jason wants to send an encrypted message. So the first thing Jason does is go to a Certificate Authority and get a Digital Certificate. This Certificate has two parts, a Public Key and a Private Key.

If Jason wants to receive and send encrypted messages with his friend Kira, they must first exchange Public keys. If you retrieve a public key from a Certificate Authority that you have chosen to trust, the key can be verified back to that certifying authority automatically. That means your e-mail program will verify that the certificate is valid, and has not been revoked. If the certificate did not come from an authority you trust, or is a PGP key, then you need to verify the key fingerprint. Typically this is done separately, by either a face to face exchange of the key or fingerprint data.

Now let's assume that both Kira and Jason are using compatible encryption schemes, and have exchanged signed messages, so they have each others public keys.

When Jason wants to send an encrypted message, the encryption process begins by converting the text of Jason's message to a pre hash code. This code is generated using a mathematical formula called an encryption algorithm. There are many types of algorithms, but for e-mail S/MIME and PGP are most common.

The hash code of Jason's message is encrypted by the e-mail program using Jason's private key. Jason then uses Kira's public key to encrypt the message, so only Kira can decrypt it with her private key, and this completes the encryption process.

9.3.6 Decryption

So Kira has received an encrypted message from Jason. This typically is indicated by a lock Icon on the message in her in box. The process of decryption is handled by the e-mail software, but what goes on behind the scenes is something like this: Kira's e-mail program uses her private key to decipher the encrypted pre hash code and the encrypted message. Then Kira's e-mail program retrieves Jason's public key from storage (remember, we exchanged keys earlier). This public key is used to decrypt the pre hash code and to verify the message came from Jason. Kira's e-mail program then generates a post hash code from the message. If the post hash code equals the pre hash code, the message has not been altered en route

Note: if you lose your private key, your encrypted files become useless, so it is important to have a procedure for making backups of your private and public keys.

9.3.7 Is Encryption Unbreakable?

According to the numbers, the level of encryption offered by, for example, PGP is unbreakable. Sure, a million computers working on breaking it would eventually succeed, but not before the million monkeys finished their script for Romeo and Juliet. The number theory behind this type of encryption involves factoring the products of very large prime numbers, and, despite the fact that mathematicians have studied prime numbers for years, there's just no easy way to do it.

But encryption and privacy are about more than just numbers. However, if someone else has access to your private key, then they have access to all of your encrypted files. Encryption only works if it is part of a larger security framework which offers protection to both your private key and your pass-phrase.

Exercises:

1. Is encryption of email legal in the country that you reside in? Find one other country that it is legal in,and one country where it is illegal to encrypt email.

2. Science fiction writers have imagined two types of futures, one in which people's lives are transparent, that is, they have no secrets, and one in which everyone's thoughts and communications are completely private. Phil Zimmerman, creator of PGP, believes in privacy as a source of freedom. Read his thoughts on why you need PGP at http://www.pgpi.org/doc/whypgp/en/. Then look at science fiction writer David Brin's article 'A Parable about Openness' at http://www.davidbrin.com/akademos.html in which he makes a number of points advocating openness as a source of freedom. Discuss these two opposing viewpoints. Which do you prefer? Which do you think would most likely succeed? What do you think the future of privacy will be like?

9.4 Connection Security

Last but not least is connection security. For web mail, ensure you are using an SSL connection to your ISPs e-mail. A small lock icon will appear in the bar at the bottom of your browser. If you are using POP and an e-mail client, ensure that you have configured your e-mail client to use SSL with POP on port 995 and SMTP on port 465. This encrypts your mail from you to your server, as well as protecting your POP / SMTP username and password. Your ISP should have a how-to on their web site to configure this. If they don't offer a secure POP / SMTP connection, change ISPs!

Exercise:

If you have an e-mail account, find out if your account is using SSL for its connection. How do you check this in your e-mail client? Does your ISP provide information regarding an SSL connection?

X

WEB SECURITY AND PRIVACY

10.1 Fundamentals of Web Security

What you do on the World Wide Web is your business. Or so you would think. But it's just not true. What you do on the web is about as private and anonymous as where you go when you leave the house. Again, you would think that it's your business and many, including ISECOM, would agree with you. However, consider a private investigator following you around town, writing down what you saw and who you spoke with. The focus of this lesson is to get you learn how to protect yourself on the web and to do that, you will have to learn where the dangers are.

The World Wide Web works in a very straight-forward manner. Once connected to the Internet through you ISP, you open a browser, tell it a website, and you get that website on your screen. However, the truth is in the details. How does the web really work? A quick trip to the World Wide Web Consortium (W3C), those fine folks who make standards for the web, will teach you all you want to know about the web. http://www.w3.org. Even the history of the web: http://www.w3.org/History.html The problem is, will definitions and standards teach you how to be safe? Apparently not. The people who want to hurt you do not necessarily follow the standards.

How does the web really work? A quick trip to the World Wide Web Consortium (W3C), those fine folks who make standards for the web, will teach you all you want to know about the web. http://www.w3.org. Even the history of the web: http://www.w3.org/History.html The problem is, will definitions and standards teach you how to be safe? Apparently not. The people who want to hurt you do not necessarily follow the standards.

10.1.1 How the web really works

The steps involved in connecting to the Internet and then to the web are very detailed even if it does seem to be smooth from the user end.

So what happens for real when you just want to get to the ISECOM website? Assuming you are already connected to the internet, here are the steps that occur in order:

1. You open your browser.
2. You type in the URL (website name).
3. Website name saved in History Cache on the hard disk.
4. Your computer looks up the name of the address to your default DNS server to find the IP address.
5. Your computer connects to the server at the IP address provided at the default web port of 80 TCP if you used "HTTP://" or 443 TCP if you used "HTTPS://" at the front of the web server name (by the way, if you used HTTPS then there are other steps involved using server certificates which we will not follow in this example).
6. Your computer requests the page or directory you specified with the default often being "index.htm" if you don't specify anything. But the server decides t's default and not your browser.
7. The pages are stored in a cache on your harddisk. Even if you tell it to store the information in memory (RAM), there is a good chance it will end up somewhere on your disk either in a PAGEFILE

or in a SWAPFILE.

8. The browser nearly instantaneously shows you what it has stored. Again, there is a difference between "perceived speed" and "actual speed" of your web surfing which is actually the difference between how fast something is downloaded (actual) and how fast your browser and graphics card can render the page and graphics and show them to you (perceived). Just because you didn't see it doesn't mean it didn't end up in your browser cache.

The history of the World Wide Web (just "web" from now on) started at CERN 1 in 1989. It was conceived by Tim Berners-Lee and Robert Cailliau who built a basic hypertext based system for sharing information. Over the next few years Tim Berners-Lee continued to develop the system until in 1993 CERN announced that the web was free for anyone to use, and the web as we know it now exploded onto the scene.

The Web is a client and server based concept, with clients such as Internet Explorer, Firefox, Mozilla, Opera, Netscape and others connecting to web servers such as IIS and Apache which supply them with content in the form of HTML 2 pages. Many companies, organizations and individuals have collections of pages hosted on servers delivering a large amount of information to the world at large.

So why do we care about web security then? Web servers often are the equivalent to the shop window of a company. It is a place where you advertise and exhibit information, but this is supposed to be under your control. What you don't want to do is leave the window open so that any passer by can reach in and take what they want for free, and you ideally want to make sure that if someone throws a brick, that the window doesn't shatter ! Unfortunately web servers are complex programs, and as such have a high probability of containing a number of bugs, and these are exploited by the less scrupulous members of society to get access to data that they shouldn't be seeing.

And the reverse is true as well. There are risks also associated with the client side of the equation like your browser. There are a number of vulnerabilities which have been discovered in the last year which allow for a malicious web site to compromise the security of a client machine making a connection to them.

10.1.2 Rattling the Locks

Standard HTML pages are transferred using HTTP 3 , this standard TCP based protocol is plain text based and this means that we can make connections to a server easily using tools such as "telnet" or "netcat". We can use this facility to gain a great deal of information about what software is running on a specific server. For example :

simon@exceat:~> netcat www.computersecurityonline.com 80

- HEAD / HTTP/1.0
- HTTP/1.1 200 OK
- Date: Fri, 07 Jan 2005 10:24:30 GMT
- Server: Apache/1.3.27 Ben-SSL/1.48 (Unix) PHP/4.2.3
- Last-Modified: Mon, 27 Sep 2004 13:17:54 GMT
- ETag: "1f81d-32a-41581302"
- Accept-Ranges: bytes
- Content-Length: 810
- Connection: close
- Content-Type: text/html

By entering "HEAD / HTTP/1.0" followed by hitting the "Return" key twice, I can gain all of the information above about the HTTP Server. Each version and make of HTTP Server will return different information at this request – an IIS server will return the following :

1. Centre Européen pour la Recherche Nucléaire (European Centre for Nuclear Research)
2. Hyper Text Markup Language
3. Hyper Text Transfer Protocol

simon@exceat:~> netcat www.microsoft.com 80 HEAD / HTTP/ 1.0

1. HTTP/1.1 200 OK
2. Connection: close
3. Date: Fri, 07 Jan 2005 11:00:45 GMT
4. Server: Microsoft-IIS/6.0
5. P3P: CP="ALL IND DSP COR ADM CONo CUR CUSo IVAo IVDo PSA PSD TAI TELo OUR
6. SAMo CNT COM INT NAV ONL PHY PRE PUR UNI"
7. X-Powered-By: ASP.NET
8. X-AspNet-Version: 1.1.4322
9. Cache-Control: public, max-age=9057
10. Expires: Fri, 07 Jan 2005 13:31:43 GMT
11. Last-Modified: Fri, 07 Jan 2005 10:45:03 GMT
12. Content-Type: text/html
13. Content-Length: 12934

You can take this further and obtain more information by using the "OPTIONS" request in the HTTP request as follows :

simon@exceat:~> netcat www.computersecurityonline.com 80 OPTIONS / HTTP/1.0

1. HTTP/1.1 200 OK
2. Date: Fri, 07 Jan 2005 10:32:38 GMT
3. Server: Apache/1.3.27 Ben-SSL/1.48 (Unix) PHP/4.2.3
4. Content-Length: 0
5. Allow: GET, HEAD, POST, PUT, DELETE, CONNECT, OPTIONS, PATCH, PROPFIND, PROPPATCH, MKCOL, COPY, MOVE, LOCK, UNLOCK, TRACE
6. Connection: close

This will give you all of the allowed HTTP commands that the server will respond to. Doing all of this by hand is rather tedious, and matching it manually against a database of know signatures and vulnerabilities is more than anyone would want to do. Fortunately for us, some very enterprising people have come up with an automated solution called "nikto".

"Nikto" is a Perl script which carries out various tests automagically ! The options are as follows:

-Cgidirs+	Scan these CGI dirs: 'none', 'all', or a value like '/cgi/'
-cookies	print cookies found
-evasion+	ids evasion technique (1-9, see below)
-findonly	find http(s) ports only, don't perform a full scan
-Format	save file (-o) Format: htm, csv or txt (assumed)
-generic	force full (generic) scan
-host+	target host
-id+	host authentication to use, format is userid:password
-mutate+	mutate checks (see below)
-nolookup	skip name lookup
-output+	write output to this file
-port+	port to use (default 80)
-root+	prepend root value to all requests, format is /directory
-ssl	force ssl mode on port
-timeout	timeout (default 10 seconds)
-useproxy	use the proxy defined in config.txt

```
   -Version              print plugin and database versions
   -vhost+               virtual host (for Host header)
 (+ means it requires a value)

 These options cannot be abbreviated:
   -debug                debug mode
   -dbcheck              syntax check scan_database.db and user_scan_database.db
   -update               update databases and plugins from cirt.net
   -verbose              verbose mode

 IDS Evasion Techniques:
     1     Random URI encoding (non-UTF8)
     2     Directory self-reference (/./)
     3     Premature URL ending
     4     Prepend long random string
     5     Fake parameter
     6     TAB as request spacer
     7     Random case sensitivity
     8     Use Windows directory separator (\)
     9     Session splicing

 Mutation Techniques:
     1     Test all files with all root directories
     2     Guess for password file names
     3     Enumerate user names via Apache (/~user type requests)
     4     Enumerate user names via cgiwrap (/cgi-bin/cgiwrap/~user type requests)
```

"Nikto" is quite comprehensive in its reporting as you can see from the following scan :

```
exceat:/# ./nikto.pl -host www.computersecurityonline.com

---------------------------------------------------------------------------
- Nikto 1.34/1.29     -      www.cirt.net
+ Target IP:        217.30.114.2
+ Target Hostname: www.computersecurityonline.com
+ Target Port:      80
+ Start Time:       Fri Jan  7 12:23:56 2005
---------------------------------------------------------------------------
- Scan is dependent on "Server" string which can be faked, use -g to override
+ Server: Apache/1.3.27 Ben-SSL/1.48 (Unix) PHP/4.2.3
- Server did not understand HTTP 1.1, switching to HTTP 1.0
+ Server does not respond with '404' for error messages (uses '400').
+      This may increase false-positives.
+ Allowed HTTP Methods: GET, HEAD, POST, PUT, DELETE, CONNECT, OPTIONS, PATCH, PROPFIND,
PROPPATCH, MKCOL, COPY, MOVE, LOCK, UNLOCK, TRACE
+ HTTP method 'PUT' method may allow clients to save files on the web server.
+ HTTP method 'CONNECT' may allow server to proxy client requests.
+ HTTP method 'DELETE' may allow clients to remove files on the web server.
+ HTTP method 'PROPFIND' may indicate DAV/WebDAV is installed. This may be used to get
directory listings if indexing is allowed but a default page exists.
+ HTTP method 'PROPPATCH' may indicate DAV/WebDAV is installed.
+ HTTP method 'TRACE' is typically only used for debugging. It should be disabled.
+ Apache/1.3.27 appears to be outdated (current is at least Apache/2.0.50). Apache 1.3.31 is
still maintained and considered secure.
+ Ben-SSL/1.48 appears to be outdated (current is at least 1.55)
+ PHP/4.2.3 appears to be outdated (current is at least 5.0.1)
+ PHP/4.2.3 - PHP below 4.3.3 may allow local attackers to safe mode and gain access to
unauthorized files. BID-8203.
+ Apache/1.3.27 - Windows and OS/2 version vulnerable to remote exploit. CAN-2003-0460
+ Apache/1.3.27 - Apache 1.3 below 1.3.29 are vulnerable to overflows in mod_rewrite and
mod_cgi. CAN-2003-0542.
+ /~root - Enumeration of users is possible by requesting ~username (responds with Forbidden
for real users, not found for non-existent users) (GET).
+ /icons/ - Directory indexing is enabled, it should only be enabled for specific directories
(if required). If indexing is not used all, the /icons directory should be removed. (GET)
+ / - TRACE option appears to allow XSS or credential theft. See
http://www.cgisecurity.com/whitehat-mirror/WhitePaper_screen.pdf for details (TRACE)
+ / - TRACK option ('TRACE' alias) appears to allow XSS or credential theft. See
http://www.cgisecurity.com/whitehat-mirror/WhitePaper_screen.pdf for details (TRACK)
+ /CVS/Entries - CVS Entries file may contain directory listing information. (GET)
```

```
+ /images/ - index of image directory available (GET)
+ /manual/ - Web server manual? tsk tsk. (GET)
+ /cgi-bin/cgiwrap - Some versions of cgiwrap allow anyone to execute commands remotely. (GET)
+ /cgi-bin/cgiwrap/~adm - cgiwrap can be used to enumerate user accounts. Recompile cgiwrap
with the "--with-quiet-errors" option to stop user enumeration. (GET)
+ /cgi-bin/cgiwrap/~bin - cgiwrap can be used to enumerate user accounts. Recompile cgiwrap
with the "--with-quiet-errors" option to stop user enumeration. (GET)
+ /cgi-bin/cgiwrap/~daemon - cgiwrap can be used to enumerate user accounts. Recompile cgiwrap
with the "--with-quiet-errors" option to stop user enumeration. (GET)
+ /cgi-bin/cgiwrap/~lp - cgiwrap can be used to enumerate user accounts. Recompile cgiwrap
with the "--with-quiet-errors" option to stop user enumeration. (GET)
+ /cgi-bin/cgiwrap/~root - cgiwrap can be used to enumerate user accounts. Recompile cgiwrap
with the "--with-quiet-errors" option to stop user enumeration. (GET)
+ /cgi-bin/cgiwrap/~xxxxx - Based on error message, cgiwrap can likely be used to find valid
user accounts. Recompile cgiwrap with the "--with-quiet-errors" option to stop user
enumeration. (GET)
+ /cgi-bin/cgiwrap/~root - cgiwrap can be used to enumerate user accounts.  Recompile cgiwrap
with the "--with-quiet-errors" option to stop user enumeration. (GET)
+ /css - Redirects to http://www.computer-security-online.com/css/ , This might be
interesting...
+ 2449 items checked - 15 item(s) found on remote host(s)
+ End Time:        Fri Jan  7 11:25:36 2005 (180 seconds)
---------------------------------------------------------------------------
+ 1 host(s) tested
```

Using the other options you can fine tune Nikto to do exactly what you need to achieve, including stealth, mutation and cookie detection.

10.1.3 Looking through Tinted Windows - SSL

It wasn't too long before everyone realized that HTTP in plain text wasn't much good for security. So the next variation was to apply encryption to it. This comes in the form of SSL 4 , and is a reasonably secure 40 or 128 bit public key encryption method. Using a 40 bit key is a lot less secure than the 128 bit and, with specialized hardware, may well be brute force breakable within a period of minutes, where as the 128 bit key will still take longer that the age of the Universe to break by brute force. There are however more complex technical attacks using something called a known cyphertext attack – this involved calculating the encryption key by analyzing a large number of messages (> 1 million) to deduce the key. In any case, you aren't going to be rushing to try and crack 128 bit encryption – so what can we learn about SSL HTTP Servers?

Quite a lot actually. As the SSL merely encrypts the standard HTTP traffic, if we set up an SSL tunnel, we can query the server as we did in section 1.1. Creating an SSL tunnel is quite straight forward, and there is a utility called "stunnel" purely for this purpose. Enter the following into a file called stunnel.conf, (replacing ssl.enabled.host with the name of the SSL server that you want to connect to:

client=yes verify=0 [psuedo-https] accept = 80 connect = ssl.enabled.host:443 TIMEOUTclose = 0

Stunnel will then map the local port 80 to the remote SSL Port 443 and will pass out plain text, so you can connect to it using any of the methods listed above :

4 Secure Sockets Layer

simon@exceat:~> netcat 127.0.0.1 80

HEAD / HTTP/1.0

HTTP/1.1 200 OK

Server: Netscape-Enterprise/4.1

Date: Fri, 07 Jan 2005 10:32:38 GMT

Content-type: text/html

Last-modified: Fri, 07 Jan 2005 05:32:38 GMT

Content-length: 5437

Accept-ranges: bytes Connection: close

10.1.4 Having someone else do it for you – Proxies

Proxies are middlemen in the HTTP transaction process. The client requests the proxy, the proxy requests the server, the server responds to the proxy and then the proxy finally passes back the request to the client, completing the transaction. Proxy servers are vulnerable to attacks in themselves, and are also capable of being a jumping off point for launching attacks onto other web servers. They can however increase security by filtering connections, both to and from servers.

10.2 Web Vulnerabilities

The simplicity of giving someone something that they ask for is made much more complex when you're in the business of selling. Web sites that sell to you, companies selling products, bloggers selling ideas and personality, or newspapers selling news, requires more than just HTML-encoded text and pictures. Dynamic web pages that help you decide what to ask for, show you alternatives, recommend other options, upsell add-ons, and only give you what you pay for require complex software. When we say goodbye to websites and hello to web applications we are in a whole new world of security problems.

10.2.1 Scripting Languages

Many scripting languages have been used to develop applications that allow businesses to bring their products or services to the web. Though this is great for the proliferation of businesses, it also creates a new avenue of attack for hackers. The majority of web application vulnerabilities come not from bugs in the chosen language but in the methods and procedures used to develop the web application as well as how the web server was configured. For example, if a form requests a zip code and the user enters "abcde", the application may fail if the developer did not properly validate incoming form data. Several languages can be used for creating web applications, including CGI's, PHP and ASP.

Common Gateway Interface (CGI): Whatis.com defines a CGI as "A standard way for a web server to pass a web user's request to an application program and to receive data back to forward to the user." CGI is part of the web's Hypertext Transfer Protocol (HTTP). Several languages can be used to facilitate the application program that receives and processes user data. The most popular CGI applications are: C, C++, Java and PERL.

PHP – Hypertext Preprocessor (PHP): PHP is an open-source server-side scripting language where the script is embedded within a web page along with its HTML. Before a page is sent to a user, the web server calls PHP to interpret and perform any operations called for in the PHP script. Whereas HTML displays static content, PHP allows the developer to build pages that present the user with dynamic, customized content based on user input. HTML pages that contain PHP scripting are usually given a file name with the suffix of ".php".

Active Server Pages (ASP): Web pages that have an .asp Active server pages (ASP), are database drive dynamically created Web page with a .ASP extension. They utilize ActiveX scripting -- usually VB Script or Jscript code. When a browser requests an ASP, the Web server generates a page with HTML code and immediately sends it back to the browser – in this way they allow web users to view real time data, but they are more vulnerable to security problems.

10.2.2 Common Web Application Problems

Web applications do not necessarily have their own special types of problems but they do have some of their own terms for problems as they appear on the web. As web application testing has grown, a specific security following has grown too and with that, a specific classification of web vulnerabilities. Common web application problems are classified below according to the OSSTMM Risk Assessment Values (http://www.isecom.org/securitymetrics.shtml), a specific way to measure security by how it affects how things work.

Exercises:

1. Open up google and type in "inurl:search.asp" or "inurl:search.php". With any of the websites which come up, attempt to type in the following in the search field. What happens? Try this for several sites.

2. In google, type in "inurl:login.asp" ond "inurl:login.php". With any of the websites which come up, attempt to type in special characters (@#$^&) for both the username and password. What happens? Try this for several sites.

3. Knowing the types of security mechanisms a web application may have, open your favorite, interactive website and try to identify if it has security mechanisms which conform to any of the RAV

classifications.

4. Commonly discussed web vulnerabilities are Cross Site Scripting (XSS) and SQL injection. What are they and how does an attacker use them to steal data or information from a web application?

10.2.3 Guidelines for Building Secure Web Applications

While there are many opinions and most of the details to building with security in mind come from the logic of the programmer and their skill with the programming language, these basic guidelines are also derived from materials available from the OSSTMM (http://www.osstmm.org).

1. Assure security does not require user decisions.
2. Assure business justifications for all inputs and outputs in the application.
3. Quarantine and validate all inputs including app content.
4. Limit trusts (to systems and users).
5. Encrypt data.
6. Hash the components.
7. Assure all interactions occur on the server side.
8. Layer the security.
9. Invisible is best- show only the service itself.
10. Trigger it to alarm.
11. Security awareness is required for users and helpdesks.

Exercises:

1. Give examples for any three of the above guidelines.
2. Give three types of technologies that one could apply to a web application as an alarm.

10.3 HTML Basics – A brief introduction

HTML is a set of instructions that explains how information is to be presented from a web server (Apache, Internet Information Server) to a browser (Firefox, Opera). It is the heart of the World Wide Web.

HTML can do much more than just display data on a web page. It can also provide data entry forms, where data can be entered for processing by a higher level language (Perl, PHP, etc). In a business setting this is where HTML is at its most useful but in a hacker setting, this is where HTML is at its most vulnerable.

10.3.3 Links

Links (or hyper-links) are really the heart of HTML page building. The biggest strength of HTML is the ability to link to other documents. A link, in the context of HTML is denoted as www.yahoo.com

The link will appear as www.yahoo.com on your website. This will take visitors of your site to Yahoo. Links can be checked and followed followed by so-called link checker programs. These programs search HTML source code for the tags and then create a file or index of the found links.

Spammers will often use this technique to find email addresses or contact forms they can use to spread their mass emails. Link checkers can also be used to check your website for "broken" links or links that don't go anywhere. This can happen a lot even in relatively small sites. Exercise

1: Create a link Create a link to https://kunalmaurya.com that displays as Hacker High School on your web page. Bonus exercise: Use the tool

10.3.4 Proxy methods for Web Application Manipulation

An HTTP proxy server serves as a middle man between a web server and a web client (browser). It intercepts and logs all connections between them and in some cases can manipulate that data request to test how the server will respond. This can be useful for testing applications for various cross-site scripting attacks (provide reference link here), SQL Injection attacks and any other direct request style attack. A proxy testing utility (SpikeProxy, WebProxy, etc), will assist with most of these tests for you. While some have an automation feature, you will quickly learn that it is actually a weak substitute for a real person behind the wheel of such tools.

Exercise

1: Choose your software

1. Download a proxy utility

2. Install the software according to the README file

3. Change your browser setting to point to the new proxy · This is usually port 8080 on localhost for these tools but read the instructions to be sure.

Once the proxy server is installed and your browser is pointed at it, surf around the site your testing. Remember, be sure to use a website that you have permission to test.

Once you have surfed around, point your browser to the proxy's admin page (for SpikeProxy, it http://www.immunitysec.com/resources-freesoftware.shtml) and begin testing the site. From the admin interface you can have the tool brute force the site's authentication methods or test for cross-site scripting. (Actually, we recommend using Mozilla or Firefox and http://livehttpheaders.mozdev.org/ and http://addneditcookies.mozdev.org/ together to modify headers and cookies on the fly without the need for a seperate proxy port. Not only does it really simplify things, it's a much more powerful tool set as we teach it in ISECOM's OSSTMM Professional Security Tester class (OPST).

But since you will need to know about setting up proxies for other things, like ad and spam filters, privacy filters, etc. We thought you should actually set one up for real and Spike is a good one to try.) A proxy server can be a powerful tool in helping you determine how solid a web application is. For penetration tests or vulnerability assessments, you must have a good proxy tool in your toolbox.

There are detailed tutorials available on using SpikeProxy at http://www.immunitysec.com/resources-papers.shtml.

10.4.1 Firewall

Firewalls originally were fireproof walls used as barriers to prevent fire from spreading, such as between apartment units within a building. The same term is used for systems (hardware and software) that seeks to prevent unauthorized access of an organization's information. Firewalls are like security guards that, based on certain rules, allow or deny access to/from traffic that enters or leaves an organization (home) system. They are important systems safe guards that seek to prevent an organization's system from being attacked by internal or external users. It is the first and most important security gate between external and internal systems.

Firewalls are generally placed between the Internet and an organization's information system. The firewall administrator configures the firewall with rules allowing or denying information packets from entering into or leaving the organization.

The rules are made using a combination of Internet Protocol (IP) address and Ports; such rules are made depending on the organization needs e.g. in a school, students are allowed in based on identity card.

The rule to the security guard in a school would be to allow all persons that carry a valid identity card and deny everyone else. However the security guard would have another rule for exiting from the school; the rule would be to allow everyone exit except small children unless accompanied by adults. A similar system is followed for firewall configuration depending on the nature of the organization, the criticality of information asset, cost of security, security policy and risk assessment.

The firewall just like a security guard cannot judge the contents of the information packet; just like the guard allows all persons with a valid identity card irrespective of nature of the persons, firewall allows entry or exit based mainly on IP address and Port numbers. Hence an entry or exit is possible by masking IP address or Port. To mitigate this risk, organizations use Intrusion Detection System, which is explained in the next section.

The firewall just like a security guard cannot judge the contents of the information packet; just like the guard allows all persons with a valid identity card irrespective of nature of the persons, firewall allows entry or exit based mainly on IP address and Port numbers. Hence an entry or exit is possible by masking IP address or Port. To mitigate this risk, organizations use Intrusion Detection System, which is explained in the next section.

Example of a firewall rule could be: Block inbound TCP address 200.224.54.253 from port 135. (An imaginary example); such rule would tell a computer connected to Internet to block any traffic originating from the computer with an IP address 200.224.54.253 using Port 135

Important activities relating to firewalls are initial configuration (creating initial rules), system maintenance (additions or change in environment), review of audit logs, acting on alarms and configuration testing.

10.4.2 Intrusion Detection System (IDS)

Imagine in a school that has proper security guards; how will the authorities detect entry of unauthorized persons? The authorities would install burglar alarm that will ring on entry of unauthorized persons. This is exactly the function of intrusion detection system in computer parlance. Firewall (security guard or fence) and IDS (burglar alarm or patrolling guard) work together; while firewall regulates entry and exits, IDS alerts/denies unauthorized access.

So how does IDS help? Just like burglar alarms, IDS alerts the authorized person (alarm rings) that an authorized packet has entered or left. Further, IDS can also instantly stop such access or user from entering or exiting the system by disabling user or access. It can also activate some other script; IDS can for example prevent or reduce impact of denial of service by blocking all access from a computer or groups of computer.

IDS can be host based or network based; host based IDS are used on individual computers while network IDS are used between computers. Host based IDS can be used to detect, alert or regulate abnormal activity on critical computers; network IDS is similarly used in respect of traffic between computers. IDS thus can also be used to detect abnormal activity. IDS like patrolling guard regularly monitors network traffic to detect any abnormality e.g. high traffic from some computers or unusual activity on a server, e.g. user logged onto application and involved in malicious activity.

IDS compare any event with historical data to detect any deviation. On detection of deviation, IDS act depending on the rule created by IDS administrator such as alerting, storing such intrusion in audit logs, stopping user from doing any activity or generating script for starting a string of activities. IDS can also detect deviation based on its database of signatures – any deviation to signature is detected and acted upon this action is similar to anti virus software. IDS is also used for detection of any activity on critical resource or for forensic by quietly watching the suspect.

Exercises:

1. Are both firewall and Intrusion Detection System required in an organization for securing its information system? If yes why? If not, why not?

2. Think of an example of a specific use of firewall rules that is applicable to the front desk person in a school; does she need to access Internet? If not, how will the rule be enforced?

3. Can a student access the school score database that contains complete information on examination scores of all students. How will this be controlled? How will this be detected in case an external party using Internet unauthorizedly accesses it?

10.5 Secure Communications

Generally, the concept associated with security communications are the processes of computer systems that creates confidence and reduces risks. For electronic communications, three requirements are necessary to ensure security. A) Authenticity b) Integrity c) Non repudiation.

Authenticity: This concept has to do with ensuring that the source of a communication is who it claims to be. It is not difficult to falsify electronic mail, or to slightly vary the name of a web page, and thus redirect users, for example http://www.diisney.com appears to be the Disney web page, but it has 2 letters "i" and can be confusing. In this case, you are actually transferred to a gambling site and the communications are not safe.

Integrity: That a communication has Integrity means that what was sent, is exactly what arrives, and has not undergone alterations (voluntary or involuntary) in the passage.

Non repudiation: If the conditions of authenticity and Integrity are fulfilled, non-repudiation means that the emitter cannot deny the sending of the electronic communication.

Non repudiation: If the conditions of authenticity and Integrity are fulfilled, non-repudiation means that the emitter cannot deny the sending of the electronic communication.

The form used to assure these conditions from a Web site is called an electronic certificate.

Maintaining the conditions of security gives us tranquillity in our electronic communications, and allows to assure the principle the privacy in the cyberspace.

10.5.1 Privacy and Confidentiality

Most web sites receive some information from those who browse them - either by explicit means like forms, or more covert methods like cookies or even navigation registries. This information can be helpful and reasonable – like remembering your book preferences on Amazon.com and, therefore,in order to ensure security to the person who browses, many sites have established declarations of Privacy and Confidentiality.

Most web sites receive some information from those who browse them - either by explicit means like forms, or more covert methods like cookies or even navigation registries. This information can be helpful and reasonable – like remembering your book preferences on Amazon.com and, therefore,in order to ensure security to the person who browses, many sites have established declarations of Privacy and Confidentiality.

On the other hand, the confidentiality talks about that a subject's information will stay secret, but this time from the perspective of the person receiving that information

For example, if you desire a prize, but you do not want your information distributed, you declare that this information is private, authorize the information to a few people, and they maintain confidentiality. If for some reason, in some survey, they ask to you specifically for that prize, and you respond that if you have it, you would hope that that information stays confidential, that is to say, who receive the information keep it in reserve.

We could generalize the definition of confidentiality like "that the information received under condition of privacy, I will maintain as if it was my own private information". It is necessary to declare the conditions of the privacy of information handling, to give basic assurances of security.

Also it is recommended that you read the conditions established by the web site you visit in their privacy policy.

Exercise:

1. Review the conditions of privacy of world-wide suppliers of WebMail: Google and Hotmail and of manufacturer like General Motors motors http://www.gm.com/privacy/index.html. Are they equal? Of those, who will share the information that I give? What measures will I be able to take if they do not observe these rules?

10.5.2 Knowing if you are communicating securely

Even with conditions of Privacy and Confidentiality, somebody can still intercept the communications. In order to give conditions discussed at the beginning of this section, a layer of security has been previously discussed called SSL, which uses digital certificates to establish a safe connection (is to say that it fulfills the authenticity, integrity and non repudiation) and provides a level with encryption in communications (this is to hide information so that if somebody takes part of the information, they cannot access it, because the message is encypted so that only the sender that sends it and the receiver, with a correct certificates, is able to understand it). This layer is called Security Socket Layer, SSL, and is visible through two elements within the web browser.

The communications is considered to be safe when the web address URL changes from HTTP to https, this change even modifies the port of the communication, from 80 to 443. Also, in the lower bar of the navigator, a closed padlock appears, which indicates conditions of security in the communications.

A type of called trick phishing exists (http://www.antiphishing.org/) in which a Web mimics the page to make seem from a bank (they copy the graphics, so that the clients enter their data, trusting that it is the bank, although it is not it). In order to avoid these situations, the authenticity of the site should be verified, and checked that the communications are safe (https and the closed padlock), and to the best of your knowledge, it verifies the certificate.

10.6 Methods of Verification

At this point, you have had opportunity to know the foundations the security in the Web, the main aspects related to some of the vulnerabilities found commonly in the web servers used to lodge the different sites with which we routinely interact when browsing in Internet, and the form in which different defects in the development of web applications, affect the security and/or the privacy of the users in general.

On the other hand, you have learned some of the technologies on which we rely to protect our servers and also our privacy. However, probably at this moment, you are realizing questions such as: I am safe, now that I have taken the corresponding actions? Is my system safe? The developers that have programmed some of the functionalities that I have used in my Web site, have they taked care of ensuring aspects to the security? How I can verify these aspects?

As probably you have thought, it is not enough to apply manufacturer updates or trust the good intentions of the developer, when your security or privacy is concerned. In the past, there have been several cases in which manufacturer's patches corrected one vulnerability, but causing another problem in the system, or once patched discovered a new vulnerability. Due to this and other reasons, you will have to consider, that is absolutely necessary to verify frequently the implemented systems, in order to the system "remains" safe.

An example of these, the OSSTMM is discussed briefly below.

10.6.1 OSSTMM

The OSSTMM, which is an abbreviation for "Open Source Security Testing Manual Methodology" is one of the methodologies of testing security that is widely used.

As described in its introduction, although certain individual tests are mentioned, these are not particularly revolutionary, the methodology altogether represents a standard of essential reference, for anyone wanting to carry out a test of security in an ordered format and with professional quality. The OSSTMM, is divided in several sections. In the same way, it is possible to identify within it, a series of specific testing modules, through which each dimension of security is tested and integrated with the tasks needed to ensure security. This sections include: Personnel Security, Data

Network Security,

Telecommunications Security, Wireless Communications Security, and Physical Security, and the sections of this methodology detail security from the point of view of WHICH test to do, WHY to do it and WHEN to do it. The OSSTMM by itself details the technical scopes and traditional operation of security, but , and this is perhaps one of the very important aspects, not the exact tests, rather it presents, what should be tested, the form in which the test results must be presented/displayed, the rules for testers to follow to assure best results, and also, incorporates the concept of security metrics with RAVs (Risk Assessment Values) to put a factual number on how much security you have. The OSSTMM is a document for professionals but it is never too early to try to understand it and learn how it works. The concepts are very thorough and it's written in an easy-to-comprehend style.

Exercises

1. Patching is a common problem today where web administrators are currently needing to patch code as new vulnerabilities are discovered. Research for a case in where a new problem occurred when installing a new security patch. Discuss about the possibilities and consequences that an administrator, who has a new patch to install, realizes that this will open a breach in its system that already was resolved. Should the patch still be installed? In relation to this subject, would it matter whether you have the source code and not?

2. Go to http://cve.mitre.org and go to search for CVEs. Enter the name of a web server (ie Apache) into the search field. When did the latest vulnerability get released? How often have vulnerabilities come out (weekly, monthly, etc.)? In reference to question number one, is patching a realistic solution to security? Why or why not? What other security measures can be used if you decide not to play the cat and mouse game of patching?

3. Download a copy of the OSSTMM and review the methodology concepts. What aspects would you emphasize from this methodology? How you think that this methodology can integrate with your verifications of security?
4. What you can find out of the RAVs?

XI
PASSWORDS

11.0 Introduction

One of the principal characters in The Matrix Reloaded is the Keymaker. The Keymaker is critically important; he is protected by the Matrix and sought by Neo, because he makes and holds the keys to the various parts of the Matrix. The Matrix is a computer generated world; the keys he makes are passwords. Within the movie, he has general passwords, back door passwords and master keys – passwords to everywhere.

Passwords are keys that control access. They let you in and keep others out. They provide information control (passwords on documents); access control (passwords to web pages) and authentication (proving that you are who you say you are).

11.1 Types of Passwords

There are three main types of passwords.

11.1.1 Strings of Characters

At the most basic level, passwords are stings of characters, numbers and symbols. Access to a keyboard or keypad allows entry of these types of passwords. These passwords range from the simplest – such as the three digit codes used on some garage door openers – to the more complicated combinations of characters, numbers and symbols that are recommended for protecting highly confidential information.

11.1.2 Strings of Characters plus a token

The next level in passwords is to require a string of characters, numbers and symbols plus a token of some type. An example of this is the ATM, which requires a card - the token - plus a personal identification number or PIN. This is considered more secure, because if you lack either item, you are denied access.

11.1.3 Biometric Passwords

The third level in passwords is the biometric password. This is the use of non-reproducible biological features, such as fingerprints or facial features to allow access. An example of this is the retinal scan, in which the retina – which is the interior surface of the back of the eye – is photographed. The retina contains a unique pattern of blood vessels that are easily seen and this pattern is compared to a reference. Biometric passwords are the most sophisticated and are considered 'safer' but in reality a password that you 'carry' in your finger or eye is no safer than a strong password that you carry in your head, provided that the software that uses the password is correctly configured.

11.2 History of Passwords

Trivia in Password History: In older versions of MS Excel and Word, passwords were stored as plain text in the document header information. View the header and you could read the password.

This is valid for all versions older than Office 2000. Windows once stored passwords as plain text in a hidden file. Forget your password? You could just delete the hidden file, and the password was erased. Early on, Microsoft and Adobe both used passwords to mean that a file was password protected when opened with their applications.

If you opened it with another application, such as Notepad, the password wasn't necessary. Microsoft Access 2.0 databases could be opened as a text file easily by just renaming them with a ".txt" extension. Doing this allowed you to see the database data. Adobe PDF files in versions 4.0 and older were printable and often viewable using Linux PDF readers or Ghostview for Windows.

Wireless networks have a problem with encryption as the key for the encryption can be guessed once you collect enough encrypted data out of the air to find the patterns and guess the keys. With todays computing power in the normal home, the key can be cracked almost immediately to find the password. Bluetooth security is considered very secure, once it is setup.

The problem is that bluetooth transmits a unique, freshly generated, password between the devices to establish the connection and the password is sent as plain text. If that password is intercepted, all future transmissions for that session can be easily decoded.

Exercise:

Download a PDF file off the Internet and try opening it with other programs. How is the data viewable?

11.4 Password Encryption

People don't usually discuss password encryption, because there seems to be no options to discuss – passwords are, by definition, encrypted. While this is usually true, encryption is not a simple yes or no proposition.

The effectiveness of encryption, usually described as its strength, ranges from very weak to extremely robust. At its weakest, we have passwords that have been simply encoded. This produces a password that is not readable directly, but, given the key, we could easily translate it using a computer, pen and paper, or a plastic decoder ring from a cereal box.

An example of this is the ROT13 cypher. ROT13 replaces every letter in a text with the letter that is 13 places away from it in the alphabet. For example 'ABC' becomes 'NOP'. Even when using algorithms that can more accurately be called encryption, the encryption is weak, if the key used to generate it is weak. Using ROT13 as an example, if you consider the 13 place differential to be the key, then ROT13 has an extremely weak key. ROT13 can be strengthened by using a different key.

You could use ROT10, replacing each letter with the one ten places forward, or you could use ROT-2, replacing each letter with the one two places before it. You could strengthen it even more, by varying the differential, such as ROTpi, where the first letter is shifted 3 places; the second, 1 place; the third, 4 places; the fourth, 1 place; and so on, using pi (3.14159265...) to provide a constantly varying differential. Because of these possible variations, when you are encrypting any type of information, you must be sure that you are using a reliable method of encryption and that the key – your contribution to the encryption – will provide you with a robust result.

You must also remember that a good system of encryption is useless without good passwords, just as good passwords are useless without good encryption.

Exercises:

1. Here is a list of fruits encoded using the ROT13 cypher. Try to decode them:

a) nccyr

b) benatr

c) yrzba

d) jngrezryba

e) gbzngb

2. Find a web page that will allow you to decode the ROT13 encoded words automatically.

3. There are many different systems that are called encryption, but the truth is that many of these are simple encoding methods. A true encryption requires a password, called a key, in order to be encoded or decoded. Of the following systems, which ones are true methods of encryption and which ones are simple codes?

a) Twofish

b) MIME

c) RSA 9 LESSON 11 - PASSWORDS

d) CAST

e) AES

f) BASE64

g) IDEA

h) TripleDES

i) ROT13

j) TLS

11.5 Password Cracking (Password Recovery)

Password cracking for illegal purposes is illegal. But if it is your password, then it's your information. Once you password protect something, and then forget your password, you are stuck.

Hence password recovery. Password cracking consists of a few basic techniques "Looking around": passwords are often taped to the bottom of keyboards, under mousepads, posted on personal bulletin boards. Brute force: just keep trying passwords until one works Automated dictionary attacks: these programs run through a series of possible dictionary words until one works as a password.

There are many programs available on the web to assist with password recovery on documents. However, newer versions of programs are becoming more and more secure, and therefore, more and more difficult to obtain passwords using the techniques above, or using password recovery software.

11.6 Protection from Password Cracking

Here are some suggestions on how to keep your passwords from being cracked:

1. Use strong passwords that cannot be determined by a dictionary attack.

2. Don't post your passwords near your computer.

3.Limit wrong attempts to three tries, then lock the account. The password must then be reset. (This does not apply to documents or password protected zip files – they do not have lock out options.)

4.Change passwords regularly.

5. Use a variety of passwords for different computers. Does this mean that you need to create a unique password for everything? Absolutely not. Maintain a master password for things that don't matter to you (perhaps the account you were required to create for TheSIMS.com or for your account on the local newspaper). But use good passwords for anything that actually needs to be secure.

Exercise:

Discuss with the class the recommendations found in **http://www.securitystats.com/tools/password.php**

XII

INTERNET LEGALITIES AND ETHICS

12.1. Introduction

New technologies, while building a new paradigm that invades every human activity, also influence the dark side of these activities: criminal behavior of individuals and of organized groups. For this reason,

we have reserved the last lesson of HHS to analyze some aspects related to Legality and Ethics, analyzing several behaviors that could end in crimes and the consequences of these crimes.

12.2. Foreign crimes versus local rights

As noted above, the introduction of new technologies can result in the creation of new dark sides of activities: criminal behavior of individuals or organized groups. There are two main characteristics through which Information Technology and Communications

(TIC's) are related to crime:

1. Technologies can give the possibility of renewing traditional ways of breaking the law. These are illegal activities which traditionally appear in the penal codes, but are now being attempted in new ways. Examples include money laundering and illegal types of pornography.

2. In addition, because of their own innovation, TIC's are resulting in the appearance of new types of criminal activities, and because of their nature, these new crimes are in the process of being added to the legislation of several countries. Examples include the distribution of spam and virus attacks.

Another characteristic of the TICs which must be emphasized is their territorial displacement, which affects the general surroundings but without any doubt affects other countries as well. Previously, areas of 'law' always had a clear territory regarding the judicial authority judging (COMPETENT JURISDICTION) and also regarding the law to be applied in the judging (APPLICABLE LAW). Both concepts are still noticeably geographic.

In summary, we can say that the TICs are global and essentially multi-border, while the law and the courts are limited to a specific state or territory. In addition, this disorientation is even more confusing than it initially appears. Although we are not aware of it, a bidirectional online communication between a user in Barcelona and a Web site hosted in an ISP in California can pass through more than 10 ISPs, hosted in a variety of remote points around the world. Facing this diversity of addresses and nationalities, it becomes necessary to ask What laws of which country will be applied in case of litigation? Which of the possible countries will be the suitable court to adjudicate the case?

The relatively recent European Council's agreement on cyber-crime was signed in November 2001 in Budapest by almost 30 countries, including the 15 partners of the European Union, the United States, Canada, Japan and South Africa. This agreement intends to restore the TERRITORIAL PRINCIPLE to define competent jurisdiction. The signing of this agreement is the culmination of four years of work that have resulted in a document containing 48 articles that are organized into four categories:

1. Infractions against confidentiality
2. Falsification and computer science fraud
3. Infractions relative to contents
4. Violations of intellectual property

Once the especially complex regulations and sanctions on criminal activity on the Internet have been described, consensus must to reached on three main areas of concerns or difficulties:

1st DIFFICULTY: JURISDICTION CONFLICT. Election of the most competent court for judging multinational and multi-border crimes. This problem is not definitively solved by any of the known judicial systems.

2nd DIFFICULTY: CONFLICT OF LAWS. Once the court has been chosen, the first obstacle that the court will encounter is choosing the law applicable for the case to be judged. Again we are forced to conclude that traditional legal criteria are not designed for the virtual surroundings.

3rd DIFFICULTY: EXECUTION OF SENTENCE. Once the competent court has determined a sentence, the sentence must be carried out, possibly by a different country than the country which dictated the sentence. Therefore, it is necessary to have an international commitment to recognition and acceptance of any sentences imposed. This problematic issue is even more complicated to solve than the two previous ones.

These complications were clearly demonstrated in the recent case of a hacker in Russia, who had hacked several US systems, and was invited to a phony US company for an interview. During the interview, he demonstrated his skills by hacking into his own network in Russia. It turned out that the interview was actually conducted by the FBI, and he was arrested. The FBI used sniffers placed on the interview computer to raid the hacker's computer in Russia and download evidence that was used to convict him.

But there are many unresolved issues:

- Was it legal for the FBI to examine the contents of a computer in Russian, without obtaining permission from the Russian government?
- By inviting the hacker to the US, the FBI did not have to arrange for his extradition to the US. Was this legal?
- Could the US convict a person for crimes that were technically committed on Russian soil?

Was it legal for the FBI to examine the contents of a computer in Russian, without obtaining permission from the Russian government? • By inviting the hacker to the US, the FBI did not have to arrange for his extradition to the US. Was this legal? • Could the US convict a person for crimes that were technically committed on Russian soil?

Exercise:

Conduct a modified white-hat / black-hat discussion of at least one of these questions (examination of a computer on foreign soil; invitation or entrapment(?) to avoid extradition; conviction for internet crimes committed against a country from foreign soil).

1. First, have students focus on and list reasons why the chosen topic was probably legal.
2. Then reverse and have them focus on and list why the chosen topic was probably illegal.
3. After these completely separate discussions, see if the class can reach a decision.

Note – these questions are interesting for discussion. There is no right answers, and governments are still working to come to a consensus on these and other issues related to the international nature of these crimes. This exercise is purely for critically examining and thinking about internet crimes, as well as formulating a logical argument for an opinion related to internet crimes.

12.3. Crimes related to the TICs

The classifications of the criminal behaviors is one of the essential principles in the penal systems. For this reason, several countries must think of changes to their penal codes, such as Spain, where the effective Penal Code was promulgated relatively recently. The well known Belloch Penal Code was approved on November 23rd 1995 (Organic Law from the Penal Code 10/1995) and it recognizes the need to adapt the penal criteria to the present social reality.

Among others, we can classify potential criminal actions into the following six sections.

1. Manipulation of data and information contained in files or on other computer devices.

2. Access to data or use of data without authorization.

3. Insertion of programs/routines in other computers to destroy or modify information, data or applications.

4. Use of other people's computers or applications without explicit authorization, with the purpose of obtaining benefits for oneself and/or harming others.

5. Use of the computer with fraudulent intentions.

6. Attacks on privacy, by means of the use and processing of personal data with a different purpose from the authorized one.

The technological crime is characterized by the difficulties involved in discovering it, proving it and prosecuting it. The victims prefer to undergo the consequences of the crime and to try to prevent it in the future rather than initiate a judicial procedure.

This situation makes is very difficult to calculate the number of such crimes committed and to plan for preventive legal measures. This is complicated by the constantly changing technologies. However, laws are changing to increasingly add legal tools of great value to judges, jurists and lawyers punish crimes related to the TICs.

Next we will analyze some specific crimes related to the TIC's.

1. Misrepresentation: The anonymity of the internet allows users to pretend to be anyone that they want to be. As a result, crimes

can be committed when users pretend to be someone else to gain information, or to gain the trust of other individuals.

2. Interception of communications: Interceptions of secrets or private communications, such as emails, or cell phone transmissions, using listening devices, recording, or reproduction of sounds and or images.

3. Discovery and revelation of secrets: Discovering company secrets by illegally examining data, or electronic documents. In some cases, the legal sentences are extended if the secrets are disclosed to a third party.

4. Unauthorized access to computers: Illegal access to accounts and information, with the intent of profiting. This includes identify theft.

5. Damaging computer files: Destroying, altering, making unusable of in any other way, damaging electronic data, programs, or document on other computers, networks or systems.

6. Illegal copying: Illegal copying of copy-righted materials, literary, artistic, scientific works through any means without the authorization of the owners of the intellectual property or its assignees.

Exercise:

1. Choose one of the topics above, and conduct the following searches:

- Find a legal case which can be classified as the chosen type of crime.
- Was there a legal judgment, and if there was, what sentence was applied ?
- Why did the authors commit this crime?

2. Regarding intellectual property: Are the following actions a crime?

- Photocopy a book in its totality
- To copy a music CD that we have not bought
- To make a copy of a music CD you have bought

- To download music MP3, or films in DIVX from Internet
- What if it were your music or movie that you were not getting royalties for? What if it were your artwork, that others were copying and stating that they created it?

12.4. Prevention of Crimes and Technologies of double use

The only reliable way to be prepared for criminal aggression in the area of the TICs is to reasonably apply the safety measures that have been explained throughout the previous HHS lessons. Also it is extremely important for the application of these measures to be done in a way that it becomes practically impossible to commit any criminal or doubtful behaviors.

It is important to note that technologies can have multiple uses and the same technique used for security can, simultaneously, result in criminal activity. This is called TECHNOLOGIES OF DOUBLE USE, whose biggest components are cryptography and technologies used to intercept electronic communications. This section discusses the reality of this phenomenon and its alarming consequences at all levels of the human activity including policy, social, economic and research.

12.4.1. The global systems of monitoring: concept "COMINT"

The term COMINT was created recently as a result of the integration of the terms "COMmunications INTelligence" and refers to the interception of communications that has resulted from the development and the massive implementation of the TIC's. Nowadays, COMINT represents a lucrative economic activity providing clients, both private and public, with intelligent contents on demand, especially in the areas of diplomacy, economy and research. This has resulted in the displacement of the obsolete scheme of military espionage with the more or less open implementation of new technologies for the examination and collection of data. The most representative examples of COMINT technologies are the systems "ECHELON" and "CARNIVORE" which are discussed next.

12.4.2. "ECHELON" System

The system has its origins in 1947, just after World War II, in an agreement between the UK and USA with clear military and security purposes. The details of this agreement are still not completely known. Later, countries like Canada, Australia and New Zealand joined the agreement, working as information providers and subordinates. The system works by indiscriminately intercepting enormous amounts of communications, no matter what means is used for transport and storage, mainly emphasizing the following listening areas:

- Broadband transmissions (wideband and Internet)
- Facsimile and telephone communications by cable: interception of cables, and submarines by means of ships equipped for this
- Cell phone communications
- Voice Recognition Systems
- Biometric System Recognition such as facial recognition via anonymous filming

Later, the valuable information is selected according to the directives in the Echelon System, with the help of several methods of Artificial Intelligence (AI) to define and apply KEY WORDS. Each one of the five member countries provides "KEY WORD DICTIONARIES" which are introduced in the communication interception devices and act as an "automatic filter". Logically, the "words" and the "dictionaries" change over time according to the particular interests of the member countries of the System. At first, ECHELON had clear military and security purposes.

Later, it became a dual system officially working for the prevention of the international organized crime (terrorism, mobs, trafficking in arms and drugs, dictatorships, etc.) but with an influence reaching Global Economy and Commercial Policies in companies.

Lately, ECHELON has been operating with a five-point star structure around two main areas. Both are structures of the NSA (National Security Agency): one in the United States, coinciding with their headquarters in Fort Meade (Maryland), and another one in England, to the north of Yorkshire, known like Meanwith Hill.

The points of the star are occupied by the tracking stations of the collaborating partners:

- The USA (2): Sugar Grove and Yakima.
- New Zealand (1): Wai Pai.
- Australia (1): Geraldtown.
- UK (1): Morwenstow (Cornwell).
- There was another one in Hong Kong before the territory was returned to China.

12.4.3. The "CARNIVORE" system

The second great global systems of interception and espionage is the one sponsored by the US FBI and is known as CARNIVORE, with a stated purpose of fighting organized crime and reinforcing the security of the US. Because of its potent technology and its versatility to apply its listening and attention areas, CARNIVORE has caused the head-on collision between this state of the art system, political organizations (US Congress) and mass media.

CARNIVORE was developed in 2000, and is an automatic system, intercepting internet communications by taking advantage of one of the fundamental principles of the net: the dissemination of information in "packages" or groups of uniform data.

CARNIVORE is able to detect and to identify these "packages of information". This is supposedly done in defense of national security and to reinforce the fight against organized and technological crime. The American civil rights organizations immediately protested this as a new attack on privacy and confidentiality of electronic information transactions.

One group, the Electronic Privacy Information Center (EPIC) has requested that a federal judge order the FBI to allow access by the ISP'S to the monitoring system – to ensure that this system is not going to be used beyond the limits of the law. In the beginning of August 2000, the Appeals Court of the District of Columbia rejected a law allowing the FBI to intercept telecommunications (specifically cell phones) without the need to ask for previous judicial permission, through a Federal Commission of Telecommunications project that tried to force mobile telephone companies to install tracking devices in all phones and thus obtain the automatic location of the calls.

It would have increased the cost of manufacturing equipment by 45%. With these two examples, we see the intentions of the FBI to generate a domestic Echelon system, centering on the internet and cell phones, known as CARNIVORE. The project has been widely rejected by different judicial courts in the US and by Congress, as there is no doubt it means an aggression to American civil rights, at least in this initial version. The project is being rethought, at least formally, including the previous judicial authorization (such as a search warrant) as a requirement for any data obtained to be accepted as evidence in a trial.

12.5. Ethical Hacking

Besides talking about criminal behaviors, crimes, and their respective sanctions, we must make it very clear that being a hacker does not mean being a delinquent.

Nowadays, companies are hiring services from "Ethical Hackers" to detect vulnerabilities of their computer science systems and therefore, improve their defense measures.

Ethical Hackers, with their knowledge, help to define the parameters of defense. They do "controlled" attacks, previously authorized by the organization, to verify the system's defenses. They create groups to learn new attack techniques, exploitations and vulnerabilities, among others. They work as researchers for the security field.

Sun Tzu said in his book "The Art of War", "Attack is the secret of defense; defense is the planning of an attack".

The methodology of ethical hacking is divided in several phases:

1. Attack Planning
2. Internet Access
3. Test and execution of an attack
4. Gathering information
5. Analysis
6. Assessment and Diagnosis
7. Final Report

One helpful tool that Ethical Hackers use is the OSSTMM methodology - Open Source Security Testing Methodology Manual. This methodology is for the testing of any security system, from guards and doors to mobile and satellite communications and satellites. At the moment it is applied and used by important organizations such as:

- Spanish Financial institutions
- the US Treasury Department for testing financial institutions
- US Navy & Air Force

Exercise:

Find information about Ethical Hacking and its role in IT security companies.

Search for information about the OSSTMM and methodologies.

Search for information about "certifications" related to the Ethical Hacking.

12.6. The 10 most common internet frauds

Listed below is a summary from the US Federal Trade Commission of the most common crimes on the Internet as of 2005.

1. Internet Auctions: Shop in a "virtual marketplace" that offers a huge selection of products at great deals. After sending their money, consumers receive an item that is less valuable than promised, or, worse yet, nothing at all.

2. Internet Access Services: Free money, simply for cashing a check. Consumers are "trapped" into long-term contracts for Internet access or another web service, with substantial penalties for cancellation or early termination.

3. Credit Card Fraud: Surf the Internet and view adult images online for free, just for sharing your credit card number to prove you're over 18. Fraudulent promoters use their credit card numbers to run up charges on the cards.

4. International Modem Dialing: Get free access to adult material and pornography by downloading a "viewer" or "dialer" computer program. Consumers complained about exorbitant long-distance charges on their phone bill. Through the program, their modem is disconnected, then reconnected to the Internet through an international long-distance number.

5. Web Cramming: Get a free custom-designed website for a 30-day trial period, with no obligation to continue. Consumers are charged on their telephone bills or received a separate invoice, even if they never accepted the offer or agreed to continue the service after the trial period.

6. Multilevel Marketing Plans/ Pyramids: Make money through the products and services you sell as well as those sold by the people you recruit into the program. Consumers say that they've bought into plans and programs, but their customers are other distributors, not the general public.

7. Travel and Vacation: Get a luxurious trip with lots of "extras" at a bargain-basement price. Companies deliver lower-quality accommodations and services than they've advertised or no trip at all. Others impose hidden charges or additional requirements after consumers have paid.

8. Business Opportunities: Taken in by promises about potential earnings, many consumers have invested in a "biz op" that turned

out to be a "biz flop." There was no evidence to back up the earnings claims.

9. Investments: Make an initial investment in a day trading system or service and you'll quickly realize huge returns. But big profits always mean big risk. Consumers have lost money to programs that claim to be able to predict the market with 100 percent accuracy.

10. Health Care Products/Services: Claims for "miracle" products and treatments convince consumers that their health problems can be cured. But people with serious illnesses who put their hopes in these offers might delay getting the health care they need.

Exercise:

Think about the following questions and discuss them with the rest of the class:

1. Do you think that you could have been a victim of some of the crimes mentioned throughout the lesson?

2. Here is a quote from an ISECOM board member: "In order to have the proper background to evaluate the security readiness of a computer system , or even an entire organization, one must possess a fundamental understanding of security mechanisms, and know how to measure the level of assurance to be placed in those security mechanisms. Discuss what is meant by this and how you could prepare to "evaluate the security readiness of a computer system". Have these lessons given you enough materials to get started?

3. [optional exercise for personal consideration (not general discussion)]: After analyzing the comments in this lesson, you may find that there are technological activities that you have heard about, or that you may have even done, that you never considered to be illegal, but now you are not sure. Some research on the internet may help clear up any questions or confusion that you have.

9 798886 840285

Printed by Libri Plureos GmbH in Hamburg, Germany